*LOKA some healthy Aussie Tucker
Get Cookin'*

Love Jorg + Barb xxx

FRESH & HEALTHY

THE ALL NEW

VICTOR CHANG

CARDIAC RESEARCH INSTITUTE

COOKBOOK

Author: Sally James

Managing editor: Philip Gore

Designer: Michelle Wiener

Recipe and copy editor: Loukie Werle

Consultant dietitian: Clare Rawcliffe

Recipe analysis: Rosemary Stanton

Marketing director: Stephen Balme

Production assistants: Hedy Aladjadjian, Sam Taylor

PHOTOGRAPHY AND STYLING

Photographer: Alan Benson

Food stylist: Michaela Le Compte

Food stylist's assistant: Rodney Dunn

Styling and food credits: The assistance of the following suppliers
is gratefully acknowledged: Anderson's; Antico's Fruitworld;
The Bay Tree; Bayswiss Homewares; Demcos Seafood;
Dinosaur Designs; Empire Homewares; Funkis Swedish Forms.

Packaged by

Media21 Publishing Pty Ltd

30 Bay Street, Double Bay, NSW 2028, Australia

Ph: (02) 9362 1800 Fax (02) 9362 9500

Email: m21@media21.com.au

Published by ACP Publishing Pty Limited

54 Park Street, Sydney, GPO Box 4088, Sydney, NSW 1028

Ph: (02) 9282 8000

© ACP Publishing Pty Limited 2000

ACN 053 273 546

Printed by South China Printing Co

Film separations by Pre-Press Global

National Library of Australia Cataloguing-in-Publication

James, Sally.

Fresh and Healthy: the all new Victor Chang Cardiac Research Institute
cookbook, good medicine, 100 fabulous new low-fat recipes.

Includes index.

ISBN 1 876624 30 2.

1. Low-fat diet - Recipes. 2. Cookery. I. Title.

641.5638

Cover: Pan-seared Lime Fish with a Warm Vegetable Salad

Back cover: Pineapple and Mint Sushi;

Turkey and Garden Vegetable Terrine with Oregano and Thyme

AUTHOR'S ACKNOWLEDGMENTS

Behind every cookbook is a network of contributors just as
vital to the book as the author. I was blessed to have
a highly skilled and fun team behind the production of
Fresh & Healthy who have made the book what it is.
There are also others who helped and supported me
during the process and I take this opportunity to express
my sincere thanks.

To Stephen Balme, Philip Gore, Craig Osment, Michelle
Wiener and all at Media21, the creators and production
team, who brought all the elements together with such
relaxed efficiency, enthusiasm and encouragement. And to
Loukie Werle, a very talented food writer, whom I was
privileged to have patiently edit the recipes.

To Professor Bob Graham, Jan Savage and the Victor
Chang Institute for offering their support and endorsement.
It has been an honour to be associated with this
organisation – they deserve huge respect for their devotion
to research and reduction in the incidence of heart
disease. And Clare Rawcliffe, for once again writing
the nutrition text and her encouragement.

To Alan Benson, my favourite photographer, who can
always turn my recipes into stunning visions and to
Michaela Le Compte for her beautiful styling work. Also
thanks to Rodney Dunn for his behind-the-scenes work
preparing the dishes for photography.

To my sister Wendy for helping test a few of
the recipes and all the taste testers – Dee, Andrew, Dane
(my loyal teaser) and Elke Pierce, Jody and Noel Parish,
my nieces and nephew Jaime, Andrew and Stephanie and
Robert Tsai. Thanks for always being honest and
enduring the retakes.

To Chris at Chatswood Seafoods who generously donated
the freshest fish and seafood for me to create dishes with.
I so much appreciated the quality of the produce and his
always jovial manner and suggestions.

Finally, and most importantly to me personally, to
Stephen Andrews, a wonderful, patient and caring man,
who supported, encouraged and nurtured me through
the whole book from the other side of the world. Stephen
brought to me a new dimension in food appreciation and
recipe creation, reminding me of the significance of the
social aspect of eating. In creating many of the recipes for
him, I learned that I could go beyond my own personal
boundaries and discover new joys of playing with food
when you think of someone else – that food should be
social, fun, passionate and not confined to recipes.

I personally dedicate this book, with my love and
thanks, to Stephen.

I hope you will feel free to expand your own boundaries
with this book and personalise my recipes to bring
yourselves and loved ones more pleasure and discoveries.

Enjoy always – life is too short to deny yourself
fun and pleasure.

FRESH & HEALTHY

THE ALL NEW

VICTOR CHANG

CARDIAC RESEARCH INSTITUTE

COOKBOOK

Sally James

PHOTOGRAPHY BY ALAN BENSON

STYLING BY MICHAELA LE COMPTE

contents

introduction

"Conscience: the only part that feels bad when the rest of you feels good."

We would like to take this opportunity to thank all who bought our first cookbook, *Simply Healthy*. Your response to this collection of mouth-watering yet healthy recipes was simply overwhelming and totally unanticipated. Clearly, the efforts of the team who developed the book, including, in particular, nutritionist and chef extraordinaire Sally James, were widely appreciated, as *Simply Healthy* was not only a best-seller but was selected from 1500 entries at the 1999 Versailles World Cookbook Fair as the winner of the Best Health Cookbook Award.

For this reason, we have reassembled this award-winning team to create another book of delicious, nutritious and heart-healthy recipes – the all-new Victor Chang Cardiac Research Institute Cookbook, *Fresh & Healthy*.

As I hope you'll agree, Sally James, again with the help of St Vincent's Hospital Dietitian Clare Rawcliffe, working in conjunction with Stephen Balme, Philip Gore and Craig Osment of Media21 and the *Good Medicine* team at Australian Consolidated Press, have done it again – another collection of outstanding recipes that will allow you to titillate the tongue without your conscience feeling bad.

We hope you will enjoy and use this cookbook frequently, and again join us as a partner in our efforts to improve the heart health of all.

Robert M. Graham, MD, FRACP, FACP

Executive Director

The Victor Chang Cardiac Research Institute

For questions, suggestions, changes and even criticisms, please access our website at www.victorchang.com.au

the Victor Chang story

Victor Chang (Yam Him) was born in Shanghai in 1936 of Australian-born Chinese parents. He came to Australia in 1953 to complete his schooling at Christian Brothers College, Lewisham, and then moved on to medical training at Sydney University. Graduating in 1962, he became an intern and later a registrar in cardiothoracic surgery at St Vincent's Hospital. After completing additional training in England, and then at the prestigious Mayo Clinic in the US, he returned to St Vincent's Hospital in 1972 to join the elite St Vincent's cardiothoracic team that already included Henry Winsor and Mark Shanahan.

A pioneer of the modern era of heart transplantation, Victor Chang established the National Heart Transplant Unit at St Vincent's Hospital in 1984. During the 1980s, he became widely known as a man of vision, as a caring surgeon, as a researcher and as an ambassador for Australia and the people of South-East Asia. During this time, he nurtured a vision to establish an internationally recognised cardiac research centre at St Vincent's and, in 1990, he and others launched the "Heart of St Vincent's Appeal". With his tragic and untimely death in Sydney on 4 July 1991, efforts to realise Victor Chang's dream accelerated and resulted in generous donations from the federal government, Mr Kerry Packer, AC, and the Australian public. With these funds, St Vincent's Hospital established the Victor Chang Cardiac Research Institute, which was launched on 15 February 1994 by the Prime Minister of Australia, the Hon Paul Keating, with Kerry Packer as Patron and Professor Robert Graham as Director. On 27 February 1995 the Institute was incorporated as an independent research facility with the Hon Neville Wran, AC, QC, as Chairman, and, on 1 November 1996, Diana, Princess of Wales opened the Institute in its new premises.

The Institute is now a partner of the St Vincent's Campus and is affiliated with the University of New South Wales. In addition to conducting fundamental heart research, it is committed to providing excellence in cardiovascular research training and in facilitating the rapid application of research discoveries to patient care.

eating fresh and healthy

We all know what we eat affects our health, but many of us are confused about what "healthy eating" really means. The answer lies in enjoying a wide variety of nutritious foods with the ultimate goal of reducing heart disease risk factors – high blood cholesterol levels, high blood pressure, excess weight and high blood sugar levels if we have diabetes. Healthy food for the heart is healthy for all the family, and it can be simple and tasty.

eat lots of fruit and vegetables

These foods are naturally low in fat, and any fat present is unsaturated – the good type for our heart. They are also low in salt, another bonus for heart health. Fruits and vegetables are high in fibre and contain antioxidants. Antioxidants are compounds which occur naturally in plant foods and have many functions that may include helping prevent heart disease, cancer and other degenerative diseases.

All fruits are healthy, fresh, canned or dried. All vegetables are great too, either cooked or raw in salads. If you choose tinned vegetables try the "no added salt" version. Avocado, nuts and seeds are the only foods in this group which contain significant fat – but it's the healthy unsaturated type. In fact most experts encourage us to eat these foods more often because they contain other healthy nutrients which have been shown to improve heart health. It is best to choose unsalted nuts, and you will need to go easy if you are overweight.

Legumes include all the dried pea and bean family – baked beans, lentils, split peas, chick peas, soy beans and many more – these vegetables are high in soluble fibre which is known to improve blood cholesterol levels and diabetes control. The soy bean is particularly popular among promoters of good health because of its phytoestrogen content. Phytoestrogens are natural plant sources of oestrogen and therefore may be related to improving heart and bone health, as well as helping alleviate some of the symptoms of menopause. Soy drinks, tofu, tempeh, soy breads and cereals are just some of the many soy foods now available.

Aim to eat at least two to three serves of fruit and at least four-to-five serves of vegetables each day.

eat lots of breads and cereals

Like fruits and vegetables, most of these foods are also naturally low in saturated fat and high in fibre, particularly the wholegrain versions. They are also good sources of antioxidants and sometimes contain phytoestrogens. All types of breads, pastas, grains and most breakfast cereals are suitable. Aim to eat at least five or six serves from this group each day.

SEVEN WAYS TO EAT MORE FRUIT AND VEGETABLES

- Include fresh fruit or fruit compote at breakfast, or add dried fruit to your cereal.
- Snack on fresh fruit, dried fruit or a fruit snack-pack during the day.
- Add lots of salad to your sandwich at lunch, or choose a side salad with your meal.
- Eat lots of vegetables or salad at your main meal and finish with a fruit-based dessert.
- Try one of the delicious legume or tofu recipes in this book.
- Sprinkle toasted nuts and seeds on your cereal, over a salad or incorporate in a recipe.
- Spread your bread with avocado or toss it through a salad.

choose lean meats and poultry, and eat fish more often

There is no need to avoid meats and poultry, but go easy on your serve size. Lean meats and poultry without the skin are excellent sources of iron and zinc. Ideally the meat/poultry should only take up about a quarter to a fifth of your plate at the main meal – vegetables should take up the rest. Seafood is a great alternative. The fats in fish are known to be heart-healthy, and most experts would recommend that you eat fish at least two to three times a week. Canned fish is also suitable. There are some wonderful fish recipes in this book.

Eggs are also very nutritious. You only need to limit them if you have a high blood cholesterol level, in which case two to three a week is quite acceptable.

choose reduced-fat and low-fat dairy foods

Dairy foods are your best source of calcium – important for bone health. The lower-fat versions are preferable since most of the fat in full-cream dairy foods is saturated. Aim to eat two to three serves of low fat dairy foods each day. Remember the low-fat versions of dairy foods have just as much calcium in them, often more than their full-cream counterparts

fats and oils

The types and amounts of fat/oil you use as a spread and in cooking are important. The better choices are those labelled polyunsaturated or monounsaturated. Grapeseed, safflower, and many margarines are polyunsaturated, while olive and canola are monounsaturated. These types of fats help lower blood cholesterol levels and have other heart-health benefits. If you are overweight be more conscious about the quantities you use – all types of fat are high in kilojoules/calories. Try mustard, ricotta, jam or chutney for a lower-fat change.

Recently, research has identified plant sterols to be particularly effective in lowering blood cholesterol levels. There are now margarines available which have been enriched with plant sterols. Although expensive, these spreads are effective in relatively small quantities (4–6 teaspoons daily). This food may be suited more specifically to those with a high blood cholesterol, rather than the whole family.

indulgences

These are the foods we dream about but feel guilty when we do indulge. The news isn't all bad. Most lollies and sweets are not high in fat which means they can be eaten. But they are not high in nutritional value either and therefore recommended in moderation. Chocolate can be hard to resist, and although it is high in saturated fat, it does not seem to elevate blood cholesterol levels as expected. However, studies have unfortunately shown that the type of fat in chocolate is not good for heart-health for other reasons. Enjoy chocolate on special occasions.

Unfortunately, most commercial cakes, pastries and biscuits contain a saturated fat called palm oil – the label commonly states "vegetable oil". Palm oil and coconut are the only vegetable foods high in saturated fat. Look for a low-fat biscuit/cake, or one where the label clearly states some sort of unsaturated fat is used. Alternatively bake your own, knowing you are using the right type of fat. Try one of the yummy recipes in this book.

Healthy-heart eating means variety and moderation. Go easy on fats, especially saturated fats, and also salt. Eat lots of fruit, vegetables, wholegrain breads and cereals. Balance your food intake with physical activity. Avoid being too restrictive, and above all else enjoy.

Many snack foods and takeaway foods are high in saturated fat. Again, palm oil is commonly used, or sometimes beef tallow. These foods tend also to be high in salt. Rather than potato crisps, corn chips and fried takeaway foods, choose healthier options such as wholesome sandwiches, fruit, yoghurt or nuts.

Many people are eating out more often than ever before. When you go to a restaurant, choose sensibly and don't be shy about asking for a healthier option even if it is not on the menu.

How often you indulge in these foods is difficult to quantify. You are probably better allowing yourself a treat now and again, rather than being too restrictive, which may eventually result in a serious over-indulgence!

alcohol

If you drink alcohol, limit your intake. Small amounts of alcohol can improve heart health by increasing the levels of HDL cholesterol i.e. the "good" type of cholesterol in your blood. Red wine seems to have additional benefits, possibly because it contains more antioxidants. However, for those who dislike red wine there are plenty of antioxidants in fruit and vegetables. Tea is also a good source of antioxidants.

You only need small amounts of alcohol to achieve these benefits. One or two standard alcoholic drinks a day (eg 1–2 small glasses of wine) are sufficient. Drinking too much alcohol can lead to high blood pressure, diabetes, liver problems, heart failure, an increased risk of certain types of cancer, and can contribute to being overweight.

salt

Try to choose low-salt foods and use salt sparingly. Eating too much salt can contribute to high blood pressure (hypertension) in some people. Most Australians eat too much salt and the majority comes from processed foods.

How to eat less salt:
• Choose fresh foods where possible – fresh fruit and vegetables, fresh meat and fish. These foods are naturally low in salt.
• When buying processed foods, try to choose those with less salt – labelled "no added salt" or "reduced salt", especially foods eaten most often, such as bread, margarine and canned foods.
• Go easy on salt added in cooking and at the table.
• Try some of the ideas in "Focus on Flavour" on page 156.

Some of the recipes in this book use a stock. Most commercial soup stocks are fairly high in salt – you may be able to find a lower-salt version in your supermarket or health food shop. Alternatively make your own, using meat, chicken or fish bones as a base with added vegetables, herbs and perhaps wine. For convenience, make it in bulk, concentrate it and freeze it in ice-cube trays.

– Clare Rawcliffe

FOUR HINTS TO KEEP IT HEALTHY

• Choose a low-fat milk.
• Choose a low-fat yoghurt, plain or flavoured.
• Choose a cheese with 15g fat per 100g or less, such as ricotta, cottage and bocconcini. There are also several brands of processed cheese slices that are low in fat.
• Choose an ice-cream with 5g fat per 100g or less.

KEEP ACTIVE

Physical activity improves heart health and helps maintain a healthy body weight. Many people have difficulty keeping their weight within the healthy range. The wide availability of too many fatty foods that smell and taste good is too hard to resist for many of us. Furthermore, the growing trend of "automation" means that it becomes easier to move about less. Following the healthy eating principles on these pages and incorporating regular physical activity into our schedules are vital steps for good health. Simple things like using the stairs rather than the lift can add "movement" into your day with relative ease.

Vegetable-crusted Honey Prawns (page 12)

nibbles & starters

Vegetable-crusted Honey Prawns

Serves 4

855 kilojoules/**205** calories per serve; **7.5g** total fat; **1.1g** saturated fat; **535mg** sodium

12 large green prawns in shell

1 tablespoon honey

1 tablespoon finely grated ginger

1 tablespoon plum sauce

1 teaspoon salt-reduced soy sauce

1 carrot, peeled and finely grated

1 large potato, peeled and finely grated

1 tablespoon sesame seeds, plus

  1 teaspoon extra

1 tablespoon peanut or olive oil

Dipping Sauce

1 tablespoon oyster sauce

2 tablespoons rice wine or sherry

1 tablespoon lime or lemon juice

Preheat oven to 190°C.

Combine the dipping sauce ingredients and set aside.

Peel and devein prawns leaving tails intact. Combine the honey, ginger, plum and soy sauce in a small bowl. In a separate flat bowl combine the carrot, potato and sesame seeds. Holding the tails, dip the prawns in the honey mixture to coat well. Roll in the grated vegetables, pressing in well to hold crust in place.

Heat the oil in a non stick or heavy based pan to high and sear the prawns for 10–15 seconds on both sides to brown the crust. Transfer to the oven and bake for 2–3 minutes or until prawns are opaque and firm. Take care not to bake too long or they will be tough.

Serve immediately, scattered with the extra sesame seeds, and with the dipping sauce.

Pork and Apple Wontons

Makes 25 wontons

495 kilojoules/**120** calories per serve; **1.5g** total fat; **0.4g** saturated fat; **235mg** sodium (note: fairly high in sodium)

Serve with soy sauce for dipping. For the leanest mince, chop in a food processor to a coarse mince texture.

2 teaspoons peanut or olive oil

1 spring onion, chopped

200g pork mince

1 granny smith or other tart apple, grated

1 tablespoon currants

1 tablespoon plum sauce

1 tablespoon oyster or hoisin sauce

25 wonton wrappers

1 egg, beaten

Preheat the oven to 190°C.

Heat oil in a non-stick pan, add the spring onion and cook for 2 minutes or until soft. Add the pork and cook, stirring, for 2–3 minutes then add the apple and cook until all meat is browned. Remove from heat and stir in the currants and sauces. Allow to cool slightly.

Lay a wonton wrapper on a clean dry surface with a corner facing you. Place about ½ tablespoon of the mince in the centre and brush the edges lightly with egg. Fold the bottom half over the top to make a triangle then bring the side corners together under the dumpling. Moisten with egg and pinch to hold in place. Repeat with remaining wontons. Place on lined oven trays and bake for 10–15 minutes or until golden brown and crisp.

and Apple Wontons

Vegetable Antipasto

A platter for 6

1385 kilojoules/**330** calories per serve; **23g** total fat; **6.6g** saturated fat; **510mg** sodium

Serve with thick slices of hot ciabatta or wood-fired bread.

Bocconcini (literally small mouthfuls) are small balls of fresh mozzarella, usually sold at cheese counters and in delis, floating in their own whey. They come in several sizes: about 50–60g each, and the very small ones are about 25–30g each, and are also known as cherry bocconcini. Very large pieces (often plaited) are known as fior di latte.

2 red capsicum, halved and seeded
2 cups diced pumpkin
3 cobs fresh corn, cut into 3 segments
¼ cup extra virgin olive oil
freshly ground pepper
4 small roma tomatoes, halved lengthwise
8 large basil leaves
4 small balls fresh bocconcini, about
  30g each
12 spears asparagus
½ cup black olives
2 tablespoons lemon juice
¼ cup balsamic or red wine vinegar
¼ cup crumbled low-salt goat or fetta cheese
¼ cup roughly chopped roasted
  hazelnuts or almonds

Preheat oven to 190°C.

Grill the capsicum, skin side up, until the skin blackens. Place in a paper bag for 10 minutes then peel and slice. Lightly steam or microwave pumpkin until nearly cooked. Place on a lined roasting pan with the corn. Brush both with a little of the olive oil, season with pepper and bake for 10–15 minutes or until pumpkin has become crisp and golden. Season the cut surface of the tomatoes with freshly ground pepper and top with a basil leaf and thick slice of bocconcini. Add to the roasting pan with the asparagus in the last 5–6 minutes of cooking, just until the cheese has melted and the asparagus is tender.

Purée the olives and lemon juice to make a coarse paste for spreading the bread, and whisk the remaining oil with the vinegar to make a dressing.

To serve, lay all the vegetables individually on a large platter. Scatter the cheese and nuts over the asparagus and drizzle all with the dressing.

Vietnamese Chicken and Mango Summer Rolls

Makes 8 rolls

670 kilojoules/**160** calories per serve; **3.9g** total fat; **0.7g** saturated fat; **140mg** sodium

juice of 1 lime

1 teaspoon fish sauce

1 teaspoon brown sugar

1 tablespoon rice wine or wine vinegar

200g cooked chicken breast, shredded

1 tablespoon chopped fresh basil

1 tablespoon chopped fresh mint

1 spring onion, finely chopped

2 tablespoons sliced pickled ginger

10 x 16cm rice papers

1 cup snow pea sprouts

1 mango, finely sliced

cracked black pepper

¼ cup chopped roasted peanuts, optional

Dipping sauce

juice of 1 lime

1 tablespoon rice wine or vinegar

1 tablespoon salt reduced soy sauce

1 tablespoon grated ginger

Combine dipping sauce ingredients and set aside. In a large bowl, whisk together the lime juice, fish sauce, sugar and rice wine. Toss through the chicken, basil and mint, cover and refrigerate for 20–30 minutes to allow flavours to develop. Stir in the onion and ginger.

Just before serving, soak a sheet of rice paper in warm water for about 20 seconds or until soft. Pat dry on each side with a clean tea towel. Lay sheet on a work surface and arrange some sprouts along the side closest to you, leaving a 3cm border at the end. Top with about ¼ cup of the chicken mixture, then a few slices of mango and season with pepper. Sprinkle with peanuts then roll up, folding in sides as you go. Place, seam side down, on a flat dish and cover with a damp tea towel. Repeat with remaining ingredients then refrigerate until ready to serve.

Serve the summer rolls whole or sliced in half diagonally, with the dipping sauce.

Pumpkin and Macadamia Soup

Serves 4

1035 kilojoules/**245** calories per serve; **21g** total fat; **3.1g** saturated fat; **45mg** sodium

1 tablespoon macadamia or olive oil

½ cup roughly chopped macadamias

1 small white onion, chopped

1 teaspoon grated ginger

2 cups diced pumpkin

1 apple, peeled and chopped

750ml (3 cups) chicken stock

whole or halved macadamias, roasted,
  for garnish

Heat oil in a heavy-based pan, add the macadamias, onion and ginger and saute for 2–3 minutes, or until golden brown. Add the pumpkin and apple and cook 2–3 minutes then pour over the stock. Cover and simmer for 20 minutes or until pumpkin is soft. Transfer mixture to a blender and process until smooth and creamy.

Reheat and serve in large bowls with a few roasted macadamias tossed over for garnish.

Baked Scallop and Mushroom Soufflés

Makes 12 canapes

165 kilojoules/**40** calories per serve; **2g** total fat; **0.4g** saturated fat; **40mg** sodium

These are perfect accompaniments to a crisp, fruity, sparkling wine.

You need only a few dried mushrooms to deliver a powerful and exotic mushroom flavour. They can be quite expensive, but a little goes a long way. Store them in airtight jars in a cool and dark place and they'll keep well for a long time. Always soak well – length of time depends on thickness – and retain the soaking water to use later in soups or risottos.

15 mushrooms (make sure 12 of them are large enough to hold a scallop, and with a deep cup)
¼ cup dried sliced mushrooms
2 lightly beaten eggwhites
2 tablespoons fresh ricotta cheese
1 tablespoon chopped fresh basil
pepper to taste
12 scallops, without roe
olive oil for brushing tops
thyme sprigs, to garnish

Preheat oven to 180°C.

Remove the stems from 12 of the mushrooms. Finely dice the remaining 3. Soak the dried mushrooms in enough boiling water to cover for 10 minutes. Place in a saucepan with the chopped mushrooms and blanch until quite soft. Drain well and press excess moisture out using paper towels. Place in a food processor with the eggwhites, ricotta, basil and pepper. Purée to a light mousse consistency. Spoon mixture into mushrooms and top with a scallop. Brush scallop with oil and bake for 8–10 minutes or until scallops are just cooked – they should still be plump and juicy.

Serve immediately, scattered with thyme sprigs.

Chive and Potato Cakes with Smoked Salmon and Beetroot Relish

Makes about 20

160 kilojoules/**40** calories per cake; **1g** total fat; **0.2g** saturated fat; **170mg** sodium

1 cup firm mashed potato (about 300g potato)

2 eggs

2 tablespoons low-fat yoghurt

¼ cup low-fat milk

1 tablespoon snipped chives

pepper, to taste

Beetroot relish

1 large beetroot, finely grated

1 tablespoon lemon juice

2 teaspoon finely chopped ginger

Yoghurt sauce

100g low-fat yoghurt

1 tablespoon chopped fresh dill leaves or
 2 teaspoons dried

To serve

6–8 slices gravlax or smoked salmon

Combine the beetroot relish ingredients and set aside.

To make chive and potato cakes, combine all the ingredients and mix well. Heat a lightly oiled non-stick frying pan and place tablespoons of mixture in the pan. Cook for 1–2 minutes each side or until golden brown. Keep warm in a low oven while the remainder are cooked. Prepare these just before serving so they are still crisp and warm.

To make yoghurt sauce, combine the yoghurt and dill and place a small amount on each cake.

To serve, cut gravlax into small strips and arrange on yoghurt, then top with the beetroot relish. Serve immediately.

Fresh Corn Soup with Crab Salsa

Serves 6

565 kilojoules/**135** calories per serve; **3.5g** total fat; **0.8g** saturated fat; **360mg** sodium

5 cobs corn (about 3 cups)

2 teaspoons olive oil

2 green onions, chopped

2 teaspoons grated ginger

375ml (1½ cups) chicken stock

2 tablespoons chopped fresh coriander

1 cup low-fat milk

white pepper and lemon juice to taste

Crab Salsa

½ cup crab meat

1 roma tomato, seeded and diced

1 tablespoon chopped coriander, extra

1 tablespoon lemon juice

Combine all the ingredients for the salsa and refrigerate until ready to use.

To make the soup, cook the whole corn on the cob, then cool slightly and remove corn kernels. Heat the oil in a large saucepan, add the green onions and ginger and saute for 1–2 minutes or until starting to soften. Set aside ½ cup of the corn and add the remainder to the saucepan with the chicken stock and coriander. Bring to the boil and cook for 5 minutes.

Purée in a blender until smooth. Return to pan, add the milk and reserved corn and season to taste with pepper. Reheat and serve with a spoon of the crab salsa.

White Bean, Leek and Celery Soup with Parmesan Croutons

Serves 4

1520 kilojoules/**365** calories per serve; **9g** total fat; **2.1g** saturated fat; **840mg** sodium

Try making your own chicken stock using leftover cuts and bones of chicken. Skim off the fat, boil to concentrate and store in ice cube trays. Not only will the flavour be a lot better, it will contain considerably less salt.

If preferred, you can use dried beans. Soak overnight then cook for 20–30 minutes before adding to soup. This would further reduce the salt content.

1 rasher lean bacon, all fat trimmed
1 litre (4 cups) chicken stock (see note)
1 leek, white part only, washed and sliced
1 red onion, chopped
1 clove garlic, crushed, optional
3 stalks celery, sliced
1 large carrot, finely sliced
1 sprig thyme or oregano
1 bay leaf
375g can white or navy beans, drained and
  well rinsed (see note)
cracked black pepper

Parmesan croutons
12 diagonal slices sourdough or
  woodfired baguette
1 tablespoon olive oil
cracked black pepper
1 tablespoon grated parmesan cheese

In a large saucepan, heat the bacon until starting to brown and crisp. Drain away any fat and add a few spoons of the stock, the leek, onion, garlic, celery and carrot. Cook over a low heat until vegetables start to soften. Add the remaining ingredients and bring to the boil. Cover and simmer for 20–30 minutes or until vegetables are very tender and soup is aromatic. Season to taste with cracked pepper and serve with parmesan croutons or just some crusty bread.

To make croutons, preheat the oven to 170°C. Brush bread with olive oil, season with pepper and sprinkle with the parmesan cheese. Place on a baking tray and bake until golden brown and crisp, about 10 minutes.

Tortilla Cones with Tuna Tartare

Makes 20

140 kilojoules/**35** calories per cone; **1.5g** total fat; **0.3g** saturated fat; **20mg** sodium

Cut the leftover tortilla scraps into shapes and bake to use as healthy chips with a dip or just to nibble on.

The longer the fish is left to marinate, the more it will 'cook' in the bowl.

2 large (29–30cm) flour tortillas or
4–5 small tortillas

Tuna Tartare

100g fresh tuna, finely diced (you could also use fresh salmon, swordfish, snapper or kingfish)
1 spring onion, finely chopped
1 roma tomato, seeded and finely diced
2 teaspoons extra virgin olive oil
juice of 2 limes
¼ cup finely chopped coriander
1 red chilli, finely chopped (or use Tabasco to taste)
¼ cup finely diced avocado
2 tablespoons low-fat yoghurt

Cut tortillas into rounds using a 7cm scone cutter (see note).

Make a slit from the middle to the outside of each round and shape into cones, securing with a toothpick. Place on an oven tray and bake for 8–10 minutes or until browned and crisp. Carefully remove toothpick and cool on a wire rack. These can be made a few days ahead of time and kept in an airtight container.

To make tuna tartare, combine all ingredients except the avocado and yoghurt, cover, and chill for at least 1 hour or overnight (see note).

Just before serving, drain away excess juice and gently fold in the avocado and yoghurt. Spoon mixture inside cones and serve immediately.

Avocado and Choko Soup

Serves 2

740 kilojoules/**175** calories per serve; **15g** total fat; **3.4g** saturated fat; **50mg** sodium

Serve with an extra dollop of yoghurt and a sprinkling of snipped chives or chopped flat-leaf parsley.

1 large choko, peeled and diced
310ml (1¼ cups) vegetable or chicken stock
½ large or 1 small avocado
1–2 teaspoons lemon juice
white pepper to taste
1 tablespoon plain low-fat yoghurt, optional

Boil the choko in the stock for 10 minutes or until tender. Transfer to a blender with the stock and remaining ingredients and purée until smooth. Reheat and serve immediately.

Chilled Asparagus Bisque

Serves 4

210 kilojoules/**50** calories per serve; **0.5g** total fat; **0.2g** saturated fat; **60mg** sodium

Serve with some fresh coriander, and extra dollops of yoghurt, if desired, and some chewy sourdough bread.

When buying green asparagus, look for crisp, shiny stems, with tightly closed tips. To remove the woody bottoms, just hold the stem with both hands and bend. The woody bit will simply snap off. Green asparagus don't need peeling, whereas white asparagus do. Purple asparagus are best left uncooked and used in salads.

1 onion, peeled and diced
3 stalks celery, chopped
2 teaspoons thyme
625ml (2½ cups) chicken stock
500g fresh asparagus, woody stalks removed and chopped
¼ cup low-fat natural yoghurt
lemon juice and white pepper

In a large saucepan, blanch the onion, celery and thyme in a little of the stock until onion is translucent. Add the asparagus and remaining stock and bring to the boil. Cover and simmer for 10 minutes. Pour mixture into a blender, add yoghurt and purée until smooth. If the asparagus is stringy, you may need to pass the mixture through a sieve. Season to taste with lemon and pepper and chill.

Mustard Pepper Salmon with Red Wine Sauce (page 30)

fish & seafood

Mustard Pepper Salmon with Red Wine Sauce

Serves 4

925 kilojoules/**220** calories per serve; **7.5g** total fat; **1.5g** saturated fat; **70mg** sodium

2 large or 4 small zucchini

4 fillets fresh salmon, about 150g each

1 tablespoon freshly ground pepper

1 tablespoon mustard seeds

2 teaspoons oregano

2 teaspoons extra virgin olive oil

½ cup red wine

4–6 large fresh basil leaves

Boil or microwave the whole zucchini until just cooked through. Allow to cool enough to slice into thin straws. Set aside.

Remove the skin and bones from the salmon. Combine the pepper, mustard seeds and oregano and press into the salmon to coat. Heat the oil in a non-stick pan and cook the salmon for 1–2 minutes on each side. Transfer to a baking dish and keep warm in a very low oven.

Pour the red wine into the pan and cook until the wine reduces and thickens. Return the zucchini straws to a separate saucepan with a little water or stock and the basil and reheat. Serve the salmon over the zucchini and spoon over the red wine sauce.

Pan-seared Calamari Ponzu with Witlof

Serves 4 as an appetiser

920 kilojoules/**220** calories per serve; **6g** total fat; **1.1g** saturated fat; **670mg** sodium

For a more complete meal, you can serve this with 2 cups cooked hot steamed rice.

3–4 calamari tubes, about 450–500g altogether

2 teaspoons olive oil

1 tablespoon sweet soy sauce

1 tablespoon each lime and lemon juice (or just use one)

⅓ cup pickled ginger, sliced

2 teaspoons sesame seeds

1 tablespoon rice wine vinegar

few drops sesame oil

2 cups snow pea sprouts

2 witlof, finely sliced horizontally

Cut the calamari into thick slices and turn inside out. Heat a heavy-based pan and add oil. Saute calamari for 30 seconds, add the sweet soy, juices and ginger. Cook for 1 minute. Remove calamari and keep warm. Reduce sauce to a glaze.

While sauce is reducing, toast the sesame seeds in a non-stick pan. While hot add the rice wine vinegar, sesame oil, sprouts and witlof. Toss quickly then remove from heat. Serve calamari over the vegetables and serve immediately.

Pan-seared Calamari Ponzu with Witlof

Lemongrass Crab on Spaghettini

Serves 4

2385 kilojoules/**570** calories per serve; **6g** total fat; **1.3g** saturated fat; **325mg** sodium

For a crunchy topping, try crushing some Japanese rice crackers in a plastic bag using a rolling pin and sprinkling over at the last minute.

Wakame is dried seaweed strips which swell up and soften when soaked. You can find it in most Asian and health food stores.

For lovers of heat, a teaspoon of hot chilli sauce in the crab can work well, but I find it can mask the subtle aromas of the lemongrass and lime.

500g spaghettini
2 tablespoons wakame (see note)
1 kaffir lime leaf, optional
8 thick asparagus spears, trimmed and
   chopped into 3 equal pieces

Lemongrass Crab

2 teaspoons olive or peanut oil
1 stalk lemongrass, bruised and
   finely chopped, white part only
1 tablespoon grated fresh ginger
400g fresh crab meat (or use premium
   canned chunk style, rinsed)
juice and grated zest of 1 lime
2 tablespoons rice wine, or dry white wine
2 tablespoons light coconut milk

Place the spaghettini in a large pot of rapidly boiling water with the wakame and lime leaf and cook according to directions on packet. Add the chopped asparagus in final 30 seconds of cooking. Drain, remove leaf and keep warm.

Meanwhile, heat the oil in a non-stick pan, add the lemongrass and ginger and cook for 2 minutes or until starting to soften and brown. Add the crab and cook, stirring for 1 minute. Pour in the lime juice and zest, rice wine and coconut milk, cover and steam for 2–3 minutes or until heated through and aromatic. Serve immediately on the hot pasta.

Coriander and Tomato Seafood Bake with Wild Rice Pilaf

Serves 4

1660 kilojoules/**395** calories per serve; **14g** total fat; **2.7g** saturated fat; **400mg** sodium

Serve with Italian bread and salad.

Wild rice is not actually rice at all: it's an aquatic grass with a delicious nutty flavour. The most expensive has long, glossy grains, but cheaper varieties, which may contain broken grains, are fine for many uses – stuffing poultry, for instance. In cooking, the outer covering may open, revealing the inner white grain, and the grains may swell three to four times their initial volume. Don't confuse this rice with Thai black rice, which is glutinous and is frequently used for sweet dishes.

1 tablespoon olive oil
1 tablespoon chopped ginger
½ cup chopped leek
1 stalk celery or fennel, chopped
100ml dry white wine
375g can chopped Italian tomatoes
½ cup chopped coriander
300g fillet fresh salmon, skin and bones removed (or any firm fleshed fish)
8 green king prawns, peeled with tails in tact
12 plump scallops
2 tablespoons grated parmesan

Wild Rice Pilaf
100g packet pure wild rice
2 green onions, chopped
1 carrot, grated
2 tablespoons chopped parsley
juice and grated rind of ½ lemon
¼ cup roasted slivered almonds

Preheat oven to 170°C.

To make the pilaf, place the rice in a pan of boiling water and cook for 5 minutes. Turn off the heat, cover with a tight-fitting lid and steam for 20–30 minutes or until rice begins to split and curl. Return to the boil and cook for 5–10 minutes or until tender. Drain, rinse, and return to pan with the onions, carrot, parsley and lemon juice and rind. Keep warm.

While rice cooks, heat the oil in a frying pan and sauté the ginger, leek and celery for 2–3 minutes or until soft. Add the wine and tomatoes and bring to the boil. Add the coriander and remove from heat.

Cut the salmon into 1cm thick slices and place with the prawns and scallops in a casserole dish. Pour over the tomato mixture and bake for 10–15 minutes or until fish just starts to flake but is still pink inside. Just before serving, toss the almonds through the rice and serve with the fish spooned over. Sprinkle with the parmesan cheese.

Grilled Whiting Fillets with Caper Salsa

Serves 4

1110 kilojoules/**265** calories per serve; **13g** total fat; **2g** saturated fat; **250mg** sodium

To seed and dice the tomatoes, insert a fork into the stem end and plunge tomato into boiling water for 30 seconds. Run under cool water then slip the skin off and cut tomato in half. Remove seeds and dice.

600g small whiting or garfish fillets, boned and scaled, skin on
olive oil, to brush
cracked black pepper

Vinaigrette

2 tablespoons extra virgin olive oil
2 tablespoons red wine vinegar
1 tablespoon lemon juice
1 tablespoon chopped flat-leaf parsley

Caper Salsa

3 vine-ripened tomatoes, seeded and diced (see note)
1 lebanese cucumber, seeded and diced
½ red onion, diced
2 tablespoons capers, rinsed and drained
½ green capsicum, finely diced
rocket leaves, to serve

Whisk together the vinaigrette ingredients.

Just before cooking the fish, combine the diced tomato, cucumber, onion, capers and capsicum in a bowl, gently toss with the dressing.

Brush the whiting lightly with oil and place, skin side down, on a baking tray. Put under a grill and cook 2–3 minutes only or until flesh just starts to flake.

To serve, spread rocket on a platter, top with salsa, arrange fillets in circular fashion on top, and season to taste with cracked pepper.

Chilli Prawns on Angel Hair Pasta

Serves 4

1235 kilojoules/**295** calories per serve; **4g** total fat; **0.6g** saturated fat; **715mg** sodium

400g angel hair pasta
750g green prawns
2 teaspoons extra virgin olive oil
1 red chilli, finely sliced
1 clove garlic, finely chopped
2 spring onions, chopped
2 tablespoons fruity dry white wine
1 teaspoon salt-reduced soy sauce
1 teaspoon sweet chilli sauce
2 roma tomatoes, seeded and diced
¼ cup each roughly chopped fresh basil and coriander
1 tablespoon wine vinegar

Cook pasta according to directions and keep warm.

Peel and devein prawns leaving tails intact. Heat the oil in a large non-stick pan or heavy-based pan and saute the chilli and garlic for 1 minute. Add the spring onions and prawns and cook until prawns start to curl and turn opaque. Add the wine and sauces and cook for 2 minutes or until mixture comes to the boil. Toss through the tomato, herbs and vinegar, remove from heat and serve immediately spooned around the cooked hot pasta.

Pan-seared Lime Fish with a Warm Vegetable Salad

Serves 4

1160 kilojoules/**275** calories per serve; **14g** total fat; **1.5g** saturated fat; **175mg** sodium

If you've never had much luck cooking fish, and would like to be eating more of it, as we all should, here is a simple, tasty and foolproof dish that will work with just about any fish. My favourites this way are blue eye, mahi mahi, swordfish and ocean trout. Be creative and experiment with your own blend of herbs and flavours. This is also great flaked through a salad or with a bowl of couscous or mash. Try with the Cucumber Raita on page 108.

4 fillets blue eye of other firm-fleshed fish, about 150g each, skin removed

freshly ground pepper to taste

1 tablespoon coriander, oregano or tarragon leaves, or herbs of your choice

2 teaspoons olive oil

juice of 1 lime

¼ cup white wine

1 tablespoon balsamic or wine vinegar

Salad

1 large carrot, cut into long batons

12 green beans or 1 bunch fresh asparagus, halved

8–10 cherry tomatoes, halved

1 lebanese cucumber, sliced

rocket or mixed lettuce leaves

¼ cup flaked toasted almonds, optional

Dressing

1 tablespoon olive oil

1 tablespoons lime juice

1 teaspoon grain mustard

Season the fish with the pepper and herbs to taste. Heat the oil in a non-stick or grill pan and sear the fish for 1 minutes or until crisp and browned. Turn over and add the lime, wine and vinegar to pan. Cook for 2–3 minutes, or until fish just starts to flake when pressed with a fork. The cooking time will vary according to type and thickness of the fish. Just take care not to go past the 'just starting to flake' stage or it will become tough and less tender. Serve straight away over the warm vegetable salad and drizzle with pan juices.

To make the Warm Vegetable Salad, blanch the carrots for 2–3 minutes or until tender-crisp, then add the asparagus and blanch for 30 seconds. Toss with the remaining salad ingredients.

To make the dressing, combine the oil, lime juice and mustard and toss through the salad.

Citrus Soy Snapper on Cucumber and Pickle Stir-fry

Serves 4

1680 kilojoules/**400** calories per serve; **8g** total fat; **1.6g** saturated fat; **315mg** sodium

finely chopped zest and the juice of 1 lemon

finely chopped zest and the juice of 1 orange

1 green onion, finely chopped

1 tablespoon salt-reduced soy sauce

1 tablespoon brown sugar

1 tablespoon olive oil

4 x 150g snapper fillets

2 cups cooked hot steamed jasmine rice

Cucumber and Pickle Stir-fry

1 telegraph cucumber

1 large carrot

¼ cup pickled ginger

1 packet snow pea sprouts (or mung bean)

Preheat oven to 190°C.

Combine lemon and orange zest and onion and set aside.

Combine juices, soy sauce and brown sugar in a small saucepan and simmer until starting to thicken. Add the zest mixture. Cook for another minute, remove from heat, add the olive oil and allow to cool.

Brush the mixture onto one side of the snapper fillets and bake, crust side up, for 8–10 minutes.

Meanwhile, cut the cucumber and carrot into thin strips using a peeler, and stir-fry for 1 minute. Toss with the ginger and sprouts and heat through for 1 minute. Serve fish with steamed jasmine rice and stir-fry.

Tea-smoked Flathead with Lemon Vinaigrette

Serves 4

1335 kilojoules/**320** calories per serve; **20g** total fat; **4.2g** saturated fat; **185mg** sodium

Serve with baguettes or crusty bread.

3 tablespoons Earl Grey tea-leaves (or try Green Tea, Jasmine or Lady Grey)

4 x 150g flathead fillets, deboned and each cut into 3–4 strips

1 ripe avocado

1 head curly endive

Dressing

juice of 1 lemon

1 teaspoon mild dijon mustard

1 tablespoon extra virgin olive oil

pepper to taste

Whisk together the dressing ingredients and set aside.

Place tea-leaves in a heavy-based pan or wok with a small rack inside. Place over a high heat and lay fillets on rack. Cover tightly with lid and smoke for 5 minutes. To help reduce the smoke entering the room, saturate a tea towel and wrap it around the lid seal. Remove from heat and allow to cool.

Slice the avocado finely and toss with some of the dressing. Arrange curly endive leaves on plates, top with the avocado and arrange fillets on top. Spoon over the dressing and serve immediately.

Prawn, Macadamia and Coriander Ravioli

Serves 4 as a large entree or light meal

1600 kilojoules/**380** calories per serve; **8.5g** total fat; **1.2g** saturated fat; **1310mg** sodium (note: high in salt, omit fish sauce if desired)

The macadamia nut, a native Australian, has taken the world by storm and not least because of its delicious buttery flavour and crisp texture. These nuts are a great source of fibre as well as oil, which is 78 per cent unsaturated – mainly mono-unsaturated – making it a healthy addition to our diet, when eaten in moderation. Macadamia nuts are expensive, so treat them with due respect. Buy in airtight packaging, and once opened, store in the refrigerator. Their high oil content makes them prone to rancidity.

¼ cup roasted macadamias, roughly chopped
1 cup fresh coriander leaves, reserve
  24 leaves for the ravioli
1 tablespoon rice wine vinegar
1 tablespoon lime juice
freshly ground black pepper
24 large green king prawns, peeled
24 wonton wrappers
1 tablespoon salt-reduced soy sauce

Stock
750ml (3 cups) water
250ml (1 cup) white wine
1 tablespoon fish sauce
1 kaffir lime leaf
1 stalk lemongrass, crushed and chopped
1 knob ginger, chopped

Bring the stock ingredients to the boil in a large saucepan.

In a small bowl combine the macadamias, coriander, vinegar, lime juice and pepper to taste. Stir in the prawns. Lay out 12 of the wonton wrappers and place a spoonful of the mixture with 1 prawn on the centre of each wrapper, topped with 2 coriander leaves. Brush edges with water or beaten egg. Place another wonton wrapper on top, pressing edges to seal. Gently slide a few at a time in the boiling stock and cook 2–3 minutes or until prawns show bright orange through the dough. Remove with a slotted spoon and keep warm while remainder are cooked.

Strain a cup of the stock into a jug and mix in the soy sauce. Serve ravioli on shallow dishes or bowls and spoon some of the sauce over the top.

New Orleans Fish Cakes

Serves 4 as a main dish

1490 kilojoules/**355** calories per serve; **9g** total fat; **2.4g** saturated fat; **925mg** sodium

As crab meat can be expensive, I've adapted the traditional American crab cake recipe to include a mixture of fish and crab. Feel free to use all crab or all fish if you'd prefer.

Serve with a garden salad, vegetables or sesame buns

If you'd like a sauce, try with yoghurt and lime juice or the Tomato Salsa with the Octopus Salad on page 50.

200g crab meat

300g boneless white fish – try gemfish, flake or ling, or ask your fishmonger

2 eggs

2 cups soft fresh breadcrumbs

ground black pepper to taste

cayenne powder to taste

1 tablespoon low-fat mayonnaise

2 teaspoons grain mustard

1 tablespoon fresh thyme leaves

¼ cup chopped parsley

1 teaspoon paprika

1 red onion, finely diced

½ cup chopped celery

2 teaspoons salt-reduced Worcestershire sauce

tabasco sauce to taste

grated zest and juice of ½ lime

2 teaspoons olive oil

Preheat oven to 190°C.

Place the crab, fish and eggs in a food processor and process to a coarse paste. Set aside 1 cup of the breadcrumbs and season to taste with pepper and cayenne. Add remaining ingredients, except the oil, to the fish and pulse on and off until just combined. Do not over mix. Shape mixture into cakes and roll in the seasoned breadcrumbs.

Heat oil in a non-stick pan and cook fish cakes for 1–2 minutes on each side or until brown and crisp. Transfer to a lined baking tray and finish cooking in the oven for 6–8 minutes or until cooked and heated through.

Flaked Trout Bagels

Makes 4 bagels

1445 kilojoules/**345** calories per serve; **4.5g** total fat; **1.1g** saturated fat; **605mg** sodium

If you find it too hard to eat the fish enclosed in the bagel, use the lid to scoop up the juices as you go along.

1 large rainbow trout
½ cup low-fat milk
1 kaffir lime leaf, optional
1 tablespoon chopped lemongrass
4 bagels
rocket or mixed lettuce leaves
freshly ground pepper to taste
1 tablespoon capers

Dressing

½ cup low-fat yoghurt
1 tablespoon fresh dill leaves
½ lebanese cucumber, grated
1 tablespoon lemon juice

Place trout, milk, lime leaf and lemongrass in a frying pan with a lid and bring to the boil. Reduce heat and simmer for 8–10 minutes, turning once, until flesh just flakes. Remove fish and allow to cool. When cool, lift off skin and remove flesh from the bones. Flake the flesh and refrigerate until ready to use.

Combine the dressing ingredients and mix well. Warm bagels in foil in the oven, split and top with rocket leaves. Arrange flaked trout over leaves, season to taste with pepper and spoon over dressing and capers.

Spring Roll-wrapped Ocean Trout

Serves 4

1230 kilojoules/**295** calories per serve; **6.5g** total fat; **1.5g** saturated fat; **600mg** sodium

Wasabi, Japanese horseradish, is very hot. Only a little is needed. Too much and your sinuses will be cleared in an instant!

Bone-removing tip – believe it or not, eye brow tweezers or any flat tipped tweezers are ideal.

4 fresh ocean trout fillets (swordfish, salmon and tuna are also perfect)
2 tablespoons low-fat yoghurt
½ teaspoon wasabi, or to taste (see note)
1 teaspoon lime juice
4 sheets nori (seaweed sheets)
4 large spring roll wrappers
1 eggwhite, lightly beaten
1 teaspoon peanut or olive oil

Salad

1 tablespoon sweet soy sauce
1 tablespoon lime juice
few drops sesame oil
¼ cup pickled ginger, sliced
2 witlof, leaves separated
½ red onion, finely sliced

Remove skin and bones from ocean trout (see note). Combine the yoghurt, wasabi and lime and brush over the fish. Wrap each fillet in a nori sheet then in a spring roll wrapper, sealing edges with the eggwhite.

Combine the soy, lime juice and sesame oil for the salad and toss with the ginger, lettuce and onion. Arrange on plates.

Heat oil in a non-stick pan and sear the fillets over a medium heat for 2–3 minutes each side or until browned and crisp. Fish should be still pink inside. Cut diagonally in half and place over salad.

Roast Swordfish with Crisp Calamari

Serves 4

1465 kilojoules/**350** calories per serve; **19g** total fat; **3.8g** saturated fat; **610mg** sodium

Serve with steamed rice or cellophane noodles.

Swordfish is popular in the Mediterranean, especially on and around the island of Sicily, where, together with tuna, it is the mainstay of the healthy Mediterranean diet. Usually available in steaks – the fish is too large to fillet – the flesh resembles that of tuna and marlin, but is much lighter in colour than those two. Cook this fish only lightly, because it can become dry when over-cooked.

1 small fennel bulb (aniseed)
grated rind and juice of 1 lemon
1 tablespoon olive oil
4 swordfish steaks (about 150g each)
freshly ground black pepper to taste
1 medium tube calamari, very finely sliced,
  to make about ¾ cup
1 tablespoon sesame seeds
1 tablespoon salt-reduced soy sauce

Preheat oven to 190°C.

Remove the tough or blemished outer leaves of the fennel and slice the white root finely. Toss with the lemon rind and half of the juice and oil. Place over the base of one large or 4 small lightly-oiled ovenproof dishes. Lay swordfish fillets over the fennel and season to taste with pepper. Toss the calamari with the remaining juice and oil, sesame seeds and soy sauce. Spoon over the top of the swordfish and spread to cover the fillets. Bake for 15 minutes, or until swordfish just starts to flake but is still plump and tender.

Lightly steam the spinach until the leaves are just wilted. Keep warm. Place fish under a hot grill for 1 minute to crisp the calamari and serve immediately.

Rice with Prawns and Wine

Serves 4
2160 kilojoules/**515** calories per serve; **6.5g** total fat; **1.2g** saturated fat; **600mg** sodium

Serve with a large green salad.

1 tablespoon olive oil
2 spring onions, chopped
1 clove garlic, crushed
1½ cups arborio rice
250ml (1 cup) dry white or sparkling wine
1 litre (4 cups) hot degreased chicken stock
600g raw green prawns, peeled, leaving
  tails intact
½ cup chopped fresh herbs (try coriander,
  basil, parsley, tarragon)
grated rind and juice of 1 lemon

Heat oil in a heavy based large saucepan. Add the onion and garlic and cook for 1–2 minutes or until soft. Add the rice and cook, stirring for 1–2 minutes. Pour in the wine and cook until all liquid is absorbed. Pour in the stock, cover loosely and cook for 15–20 minutes or until most of liquid is absorbed.

Add the prawns, fresh herbs and lemon rind and juice, cover and cook on a low heat for 2–3 minutes or until prawns are opaque and cooked through. Remove from heat and let sit for 5 minutes before serving.

Slow-cooked Octopus and Rocket Salad

Serves 6 as a light meal
755 kilojoules/**180** calories per serve; **7.5g** total fat; **1.2g** saturated fat; **270mg** sodium

I can't resist a wood-fired or sourdough loaf with this dish, but it is also great with a big dish of cooked pasta to toss through.

600–700g baby octopus, cleaned
½ cup balsamic vinegar
½ cup white wine
6–8 basil leaves
2 cloves garlic, crushed
Salad
3 roma tomatoes, seeded and diced
1 red onion, finely diced
2–3 basil leaves
2 tablespoons extra virgin olive oil
freshly ground pepper
1 large bunch rocket

Preheat the oven to 170°C.

Remove the eyes and beak from the octopus if the fishmonger hasn't done so already. Place in large casserole dish and pour in the balsamic vinegar, wine, basil and garlic. Cover and bake for 40–45 minutes or until octopus is very tender. Remove from liquid.

Combine the tomatoes, onion, basil, oil and 1–2 tablespoons of the cooking liquid from the octopus. Toss well to combine and season to taste with pepper.

To serve, place rocket leaves on plates, top with the octopus and salad.

Squid Ink Pasta with Swordfish Ceviche

Serves 4

2740 kilojoules/**655** calories per serve; **14g** total fat; **2.7g** saturated fat; **300mg** sodium

You could also use tuna, blue eye or salmon – but not frozen. Look for firm, shiny fish, not sitting on or scattered with ice, and with no brownish hue.

400g very fresh swordfish
2 tablespoons mirin (rice wine) or white wine
juice and zest of 1 lime
1 tablespoon extra virgin olive oil
2 teaspoons salt-reduced soy sauce
¼ cup chopped fresh coriander
¼ cup chopped fresh basil
500g squid ink fettuccine or preferred pasta
   (try spinach or tomato for the colour)

Remove the skin from the swordfish and dice the flesh finely. Place in a bowl with the mirin, lime juice and zest, oil, soy sauce, coriander and basil. Cover, refrigerate and allow to marinate for 20–30 minutes. Swordfish will begin to 'cook' in the marinade.

Meanwhile, cook the pasta according to directions, drain well and return to pan. Toss through the swordfish ceviche. Allow to sit for a minute over a low heat, then serve while hot. Alternatively, serve pasta with ceviche spooned over the top. Enjoy with a mixed lettuce salad and tomatoes.

Caramelised Scallops on Warm Asparagus and Tomato Salad

Serves 4

470 kilojoules/**110** calories per serve; **4.5g** total fat; **0.7g** saturated fat; **195mg** sodium

This dish was inspired by a memorable meal by chef Robert Curry at Domaine Chandon Vineyards in California's Napa Valley.

1 bunch fresh asparagus, sliced diagonally
1 carrot, peeled, diagonally sliced
2 green onions, sliced into 1cm pieces
100ml chicken stock
cracked black pepper
2 roma tomatoes, sliced
1 teaspoon brown sugar
2 teaspoons red wine vinigar
2 teaspoons extra virgin olive oil
24 plump scallops
Dressing
¼ cup vegetable or chicken stock
1 canned artichoke
1 teaspoon extra virgin olive oil
1 tablespoon lemon juice

Preheat oven to 200°C. Place the asparagus, carrots, onions and stock in a small pan. Season to taste with cracked pepper and bring to the boil. Cook 2–3 minutes or until vegetables are tender. Stir in the tomatoes and keep warm.

Dissolve the sugar in the vinegar and set aside. Heat a frying pan with an ovenproof handle and add the oil. Season scallops on both sides with pepper and sear in hot pan for 1 minute. Add the sugared vinegar, rotate pan to distribute the liquid and place in the oven for 2 minutes. Turn the scallops over then remove from pan.

Place the vegetables in the centre of 4 warm plates, allowing the stock to spread out. Surround with 6 scallops and serve the dressing on the side.

To make the dressing, heat the chicken stock and boil the artichoke for 2–3 minutes. Place in a blender and purée, gradually adding the oil and lemon juice.

Grilled Veal with Orange and Rosemary Sauce (page 56)

meat

Grilled Veal with Orange and Rosemary Sauce

Serves 4

735 kilojoules/**175** calories per serve; **4.5g** total fat; **1g** saturated fat; **120mg** sodium

Serve with rice or pasta with steamed green beans, squash and carrots, or vegetables of your choice.

2 teaspoons olive oil

4 lean thick veal steaks (about 125g each)

Sauce

¼ cup orange juice

¼ cup white wine

¼ cup chicken stock

1 sprig rosemary

pepper to taste

Heat a non-stick pan, add the oil and sear the steaks for 2–3 minutes on each side or as desired. Transfer to a dish, cover with foil and keep warm in a low oven. Add the juice, wine, stock and rosemary to the pan and cook until mixture is a sauce consistency. Remove the rosemary and season to taste with pepper. Slice the veal and serve with the sauce spooned over.

Pork Balls with Noodles

Serves 4

2430 kilojoules/**580** calories per serve; **11g** total fat; **3.3g** saturated fat; **315mg** sodium

If you can't find pork mince, buy diced pork or pork steak, trim off any fat and cut into small pieces. Place in a food processor with the egg, soy, coriander and ginger and pulse on and off until ground. You could also try using chicken or veal mince.

400g lean pork mince (see note)

1 eggwhite, lightly whisked

2 teaspoons salt-reduced soy sauce

2 tablespoons chopped fresh coriander leaves (or 2 teaspoons dried leaves)

1 tablespoon finely grated ginger

2 tablespoons cornflour

500ml (2 cups) degreased chicken stock

1 teaspoon fish sauce

4 green onions, ends trimmed and cut into 5cm batons

4 mushrooms

1 cup snow or snap peas

1 carrot, cut into thin strips

2 packets fresh udon noodles

Combine the mince, eggwhite, soy sauce, coriander and ginger in a bowl. Shape into small balls and toss in the cornflour to coat. Bring the chicken stock and fish sauce to the boil in a large saucepan. Reduce heat to a simmer and add the pork balls. Cook for 10 minutes or until nearly cooked through. Add the vegetables and cook for 2 minutes or until tender-crisp. Pour boiling water over the udon noodles to loosen and soften, then drain and add to the pan. Simmer another minute or until the noodles are soft.

Pork Balls with Noodles

Thai-cured Lamb and Noodle Salad

Serves 4

1240 kilojoules/**295** calories per serve; **7.5g** total fat; **2.7g** saturated fat; **175mg** sodium

Thai salads are all the rage, and when looking at a typical list of ingredients, it's hardly surprising. Fragrant inclusions, such as fresh coriander, mint, lemongrass and kaffir lime leaves, make the flavour indescribably exotic and almost ethereal. With a dressing of strong lime juice, pungent fish sauce and often chillies, the lightness of flavour is matched by the lack of calories. Oil is never found in a true Thai dressing.

500g lean lamb backstrap or loin, trimmed

Thai curry paste

2 stalks fresh coriander with roots

2 tablespoons chopped lemongrass (white part only)

2 tablespoons grated ginger

2 teaspoons chopped lime rind

2 teaspoons brown or palm sugar

1 clove garlic, crushed

Noodle Salad

100g vermicelli or cellophane noodles

2 bird's eye or small red chillies, finely chopped

2 tablespoons finely chopped peanuts, optional

Dressing

juice of ½ lime

1 teaspoon fish sauce

2 teaspoons salt-reduced soy sauce

To make the Thai curry paste: wash and remove the leaves from the coriander stalks and set aside for the salad. Chop the white root and crush together with the remaining paste ingredients in a mortar and pestle, or briefly in a food processor. Spread over the lamb fillet, cover and refrigerate overnight.

Soak the noodles in cold water for 10 minutes, drain well then plunge into boiling water for 1 minute or until softened and tender. Drain and toss with the reserved chopped coriander leaves, chilli and peanuts.

Combine the dressing ingredients.

Heat a grill pan or heavy-based, non-stick pan to high, brush with oil and sear the lamb for 1–2 minutes each side or as preferred. Don't overcook, or it won't be as tender. Cover loosely with foil and allow to rest for 10 minutes before slicing thinly and serving tossed through the noodle salad. Spoon over the dressing.

Sage and Mint Lamb on Pea Mash

Serves 4

940 kilojoules/**225** calories per serve; **10g** total fat; **2.8g** saturated fat; **65mg** sodium

Serve with salad
and crusty bread.

1 potato, peeled and chopped

2 cups frozen or fresh peas

2 teaspoons mint sauce or wine vinegar

8 lean lamb cutlets or leg chops

1 tablespoon olive oil

2 tablespoons fresh chopped sage, or
  1 tablespoon dried

¼ cup white wine

2 tablespoons chopped mint

Boil the potato until nearly cooked, add the peas and cook until tender. Mash with the mint sauce and keep warm.

Meanwhile, trim any excess fat and sinew from lamb. Brush with the oil and press sage into surface. Heat a large non-stick pan over medium high heat, add lamb and cook for 4–5 minutes each side or until nearly cooked. Add the wine and mint and cook for 2 minutes. Serve with the pea mash.

Maple Syrup and Apple Braised Pork with Horseradish Mash

Serves 4

1825 kilojoules/**435** calories per serve; **9.5g** total fat; **2.2g** saturated fat; **305mg** sodium

Serve with
steamed zucchini
and squash.

4 butterflied pork neck fillets
  (about 500g–600g)

2 tablespoons dijon mustard

1 tablespoon olive oil

250ml (1 cup) apple juice

⅓ cup maple syrup

1 tablespoon lemon juice

1 large green apple, peeled, cut into
  quarters and thinly sliced

3 large potatoes, peeled and chopped

¼ cup well-shaken buttermilk or low-fat milk

1 tablespoon horseradish

pepper to taste

Brush the pork fillets with dijon mustard. Heat the oil in a large heavy-based pan and sauté the fillets on high heat for 2 minutes on each side or until browned and crisp. Combine the apple juice, maple syrup and lemon juice and add to pan. Reduce heat, cover and simmer over low heat for 25–30 minutes or until pork is tender, turning occasionally and spooning over sauce. Add the apple for the last 10 minutes of cooking time.

Meanwhile, boil the potatoes until tender then mash with the milk, horseradish and pepper to taste. Keep warm. Remove the pork from pan, cover with foil and keep warm. Boil the remaining liquid until thick and syrupy. Serve the pork on the mash and spoon over the sauce.

Pear and Parmesan Risotto with Shaved Pepper Beef

Serves 4

2325 kilojoules/**555** calories per serve; **12g** total fat; **3.8g** saturated fat; **195mg** sodium

Try serving this risotto drizzled with a little balsamic vinegar and a mixed green salad. Risottos are so versatile that you can almost always find suitable ingredients in your fridge or pantry to cook one on the spur of the moment. The rice itself is important, and although there are substitutes such as barley and rice-shaped pasta, called orzo, the most common rice for a successful risotto is arborio, originally grown in the Po valley in Italy, but now also cultivated in Australia.

1 tablespoon extra virgin olive oil

1 large firm green pear, peeled and diced

juice and zest of ½ lemon

freshly ground pepper

1 onion, chopped

1½ cups arborio rice

250ml (1 cup) dry white wine

1 litre (4 cups) hot chicken stock

2–3 leaves fresh basil

2 tablespoons shaved parmesan cheese

Pepper Beef

400g lean beef fillet

1 tablespoon freshly ground pepper

Heat half the oil in a large heavy-based saucepan. Add the pear and cook for 1–2 minutes or until starting to soften. Remove from pan, toss in some of the lemon juice, season with pepper and set aside. Heat the remaining oil and sauté the onion for 1–2 minutes or until translucent. Add rice and cook 1–2 minutes. Pour in wine and cook, stirring until all liquid is absorbed. Add the chicken stock gradually, a ladle or so at a time, and cook, stirring occasionally. After 15 minutes add the pear, then continue adding the stock until rice is cooked, about 5–6 more minutes. Add the remaining lemon juice, zest and basil. Remove from heat, cover and allow to sit for 2–3 minutes.

While the rice is cooking, brush the beef with oil, coat with the pepper and pan-sear on high heat until cooked medium rare or to taste. Remove from pan, cover with foil and allow to sit for 5–10 minutes before slicing thinly.

To serve, toss the parmesan through the risotto and top with the warm beef.

Roast Lamb Souvlaki

Makes 4 souvlaki

1975 kilojoules/**470** calories per serve; **9.5g** total fat; **2.4g** saturated fat; **805mg** sodium

Goat's milk yoghurt is delicious with this dish.

2 cloves garlic, crushed

grated rind and juice of 1 lemon

400g lamb fillets

2 teaspoons olive oil

4 large pita breads

1 cup shredded butter lettuce

Salad

½ cup chopped parsley

2 tablespoons chopped mint

2 roma tomatoes, diced

½ lebanese cucumber, finely diced

2 tablespoons chopped black olives

½ red onion, sliced

Dressing

2 tablespoons low-fat yoghurt (see note)

1 clove garlic, crushed

Preheat the oven to 200°C.

Combine the garlic and lemon rind. Brush the lamb with the oil and a little of the lemon juice. Make 5–6 small slits in the top of each fillet. Fill with the garlic lemon mixture. Season to taste with ground pepper. Place on rack on an oven tray and bake for 12–15 minutes or until medium rare or as preferred. Keep warm, loosely covered with foil.

Combine the salad ingredients. Mix the yoghurt with the garlic and remaining lemon juice. Warm the pita breads in a non-stick pan for 30 seconds on each side, top with the lettuce then the salad. Slice the lamb and place on the salad then drizzle with the dressing. Wrap tightly and eat while still warm.

Grilled Steak with Oyster Ragout

Serves 4

980 kilojoules/**235** calories per serve; **8.5g** total fat; **3g** saturated fat; **140mg** sodium

Serve with toasted Italian bread or mashed potato, green vegetables or salad.

2 teaspoons olive oil

½ leek, white part washed and finely sliced

2 roma tomatoes, seeded and diced

¼ cup chopped fresh basil

freshly ground pepper, to taste

1 tablespoon lemon juice

100ml red wine or beef stock

8 oysters

4 x 125g–150g fillets or lean beef steak (try New York, scotch or oyster blade fillets)

Heat the oil in a medium saucepan and cook the leek over low heat until soft. Add the tomato, basil and pepper to taste and cook for 5 minutes. Add the lemon juice and wine and bring to the boil, then reduce heat to low while steak is cooking. Add the oysters 1–2 minutes before serving to heat through.

Meanwhile, grill or barbecue steak till cooked as desired. Serve with the ragout.

Wine-braised Veal Shanks with White Bean Purée

Serves 4

1715 kilojoules/**410** calories per serve; **11g** total fat; **1.7g** saturated fat; **485mg** sodium

Veal shanks vary greatly in size. However, the gelatinous meat is very satisfying and the most common size available provides enough meat for 2 people, so choose accordingly.

White bean purée is a natural with veal cooked in this manner, and you can choose from different varieties, such as cannellini, great northern or lima beans. Always drain and rinse canned beans well before use.

4 small veal shanks, french trimmed
flour, for dusting
2 tablespoons olive oil
1 onion, diced
2 carrots, diced
2 stalks celery, diced
2 cups halved button mushrooms
1 sprig thyme
1 sprig oregano or 2 teaspoons dried
375g can crushed tomatoes
1 cup degreased chicken stock
1 cup white wine
½ cup water

White Bean Purée
1 large potato, peeled and diced
375g can white beans, drained
¼ cup low-fat milk or chicken stock
1 tablespoon finely chopped coriander
ground black pepper

Trim and discard any fat from the veal. Toss shanks with the flour to coat. Heat 1 tablespoon of the oil in a heavy-based large saucepan and brown the shanks on all sides. Remove from pan, add the remaining oil, onion, carrot, celery and mushrooms and cook for 2–3 minutes or until onion is soft. Return the veal to the pan with the herbs, tomato, stock, wine and water. Cover and cook on very low heat for 1½–2 hours or until veal is tender and falls off the bone. Add more water during cooking if needed. When shanks are cooked, skim the top of the liquid well to remove any fat.

When shanks are nearly cooked, place the potato in boiling water and cook for 10 minutes. Add the beans and cook until the vegetables are tender. Drain and purée in a food processor with enough milk or stock to bring to desired consistency. Return to pan, stir in the coriander and season to taste with pepper. Reheat and serve hot with the veal.

Lamb and Eggplant Kebabs with Fattoush

Serves 4

1710 kilojoules/**410** calories per serve; **16g** total fat; **3.8g** saturated fat; **320mg** sodium

When cooking kebabs always make sure you soak wooden or bamboo skewers for 30 minutes in cold water before adding the meat and/or other ingredients, or your skewers may burn before the meat is cooked. Metal skewers are always at the ready and cannot burn. They do get very hot though!

Fattoush is a Middle Eastern bread salad, closely related to Italian panzanella. The main difference is in the bread used: pita for fattoush, ciabatta for panzanella.

500g boned leg of lamb or fillet, trimmed of fat
1 clove garlic, crushed
juice and zest of ½ lemon
1 tablespoon olive oil
2 tablespoons yoghurt
1 tablespoon chopped fresh parsley
1 large eggplant, cut into large cubes

Fattoush
1 large or 2 small pita breads
1 large lebanese cucumber, cubed
3 vine-ripened tomatoes, diced
1 green onion, chopped
½ green capsicum, diced
½ cup chopped parsley
2 tablespoons lemon juice
1 tablespoon olive oil
1 clove garlic, crushed

Cucumber Raita
(see recipe page 108)

Cut the lamb into bite-sized chunks and place in a large bowl or dish. Combine the garlic, lemon juice and zest, oil, yoghurt and parsley and toss through the lamb. Cover and refrigerate at least 2 hours, or overnight.

To make the fattoush, toast the pita bread in a moderate oven or under the grill until golden brown and crisp. Crumble into bite-sized pieces and set aside. Toss together the cucumber, tomatoes, green onion, capsicum and parsley. Combine the juice, oil and garlic and toss through the salad. Just before serving stir in the crumbled pita bread.

Thread lamb onto metal or pre-soaked wooden skewers alternately with the eggplant. Grill or barbecue over high heat until cooked as desired. Serve over the fattoush with the Cucumber Raita and lemon wedges.

Peppercorn Beef with Port and Mushroom Sauce

Serves 4

1070 kilojoules/**255** calories per serve; **10g** total fat; **3g** saturated fat; **110mg** sodium

Serve with baby potatoes and steamed greens.

4 lean steaks (try fillet, tenderloin or rump)
1 tablespoon olive oil
1 tablespoon crushed peppercorns

Port and Mushroom Sauce

1½ cups sliced shitake or swiss brown mushrooms (or your choice of mushrooms)
1 tablespoon pepper-seasoned flour
1 brown shallot, finely chopped, or
    1 tablespoon finely chopped white onion
¾ cup beef stock
2 teaspoons no-added-salt tomato paste
1 teaspoon reduced-salt Worcestershire sauce
100ml port or fortified wine
1 tablespoon red wine or cider vinegar

To make sauce, toss the mushrooms and flour together in a plastic bag and set aside. Cook the shallot in 2 tablespoons of the stock until soft then stir in the tomato paste and sauce. Cook for 1–2 minutes then add the port. Boil for 3 minutes or until thickening. Add the remaining stock and vinegar and bring to the boil. Add the mushrooms and cook, stirring until mushrooms are soft and mixure is sauce consistency. Keep warm.

Brush steaks with oil and roll in pepper. Cook in a preheated grill pan or barbecue, or grill for 2–3 minutes each side or as preferred. Serve with the mushroom sauce.

Stir-fried Pork and Sesame Rice

Serves 4

1760 kilojoules/**420** calories per serve; **12g** total fat; **2.1g** saturated fat; **250mg** sodium

To curl green onions, soak the green part in iced water for 5 minutes and serve scattered on top as a garnish.

400g lean pork fillet
1 tablespoon peanut oil
few drops sesame oil
1 tablespoon grated ginger
2 green onions, cut into long diagonal strips
1 red capsicum, cut into thin strips
1 green capsicum, cut into thin strips
fresh coriander leaves

Sauce

1 tablespoon salt-reduced soy sauce
2 tablespoons rice wine or sherry
2 tablespoons chicken stock
1 tablespoon no-added-salt tomato paste

Sesame Rice

3 cups hot steamed rice
2 tablespoons toasted sesame seeds
few drops sesame oil
2 tablespoons sliced pickled ginger, optional

Trim any fat from the pork and cut pork into thin pieces. Heat the oils in a wok or large non-stick frying pan and stir-fry the ginger and green onions for 1 minute. Add pork and stir-fry until browned. Add the capsicum and stir-fry for 1–2 minutes or until just starting to soften.

Combine the sauce ingredients and toss into the pan. Stir a few times to distribute sauce, then reduce heat, cover and allow to steam for 3–4 minutes. Serve over the hot sesame rice and scatter with coriander leaves.

To make rice, combine ingredients and toss lightly with a fork.

Lemon and Cheese-crusted Roast Lamb Loin

Serves 8

950 kilojoules/**225** calories per serve; **9.5g** total fat; **3g** saturated fat; **275mg** sodium

Steamed green beans, snap peas or asparagus, chats and grilled tomato are delicious with this dish, as well as a splash of balsamic vinegar over the lamb.

1 kg boned lamb loins or boned leg of lamb, butterflied
2 tablespoons olive oil
2 tablespoons fresh rosemary leaves
2 tablespoons fresh thyme leaves
juice and coarsely grated rind of 1 lemon
½ cup loosely packed crumbled fat-reduced fetta cheese
½ cup coarse fresh breadcrumbs
¼ cup fresh chopped parsley
freshly ground pepper
1 tablespoon dijon mustard

Preheat oven to 175°C.

Trim excess fat and sinew off lamb and pound lamb to flatten slightly between sheets of baking paper. Lay, with the rough interior side facing up, on a work surface. In a food processor, combine 1 tablespoon of the oil with the rosemary, thyme, half the lemon juice and the lemon rind. Process into a coarse paste. Reserve 1–2 tablespoons of the mixture and combine the remainder with the remaining lemon juice, the cheese, breadcrumbs and parsley, and mix well. Set aside.

Spread the reserved 2 tablespoons of herb mixture over the rough surface of the lamb, leaving a 2cm border around the edges. Roll lamb up and tie securely with string at regular intervals. Rub remaining oil over surfaces and season with freshly ground pepper. Heat a deep baking dish or non-stick frying pan over high heat and brown the lamb on all sides. Transfer to a wire rack inside the baking dish and roast for 30 minutes.

Transfer the lamb to a cutting board and carefully remove string. Brush with mustard and carefully press cheese mixture onto the top and sides of lamb, pressing firmly to hold in place. Return to oven and bake for 15 minutes for medium rare. Remove from oven, cover loosely with foil and leave in a warm place for 10 minutes. Carve into thick slices and serve with vegetables.

Flash-seared Teriyaki Beef on Glazed Soba Noodles

Serves 4

2055 kilojoules/**490** calories per serve; **19g** total fat; **4g** saturated fat; **520mg** sodium

This is delicious with a big cup of miso soup.

450–500g lean beef tenderloin or fillet

Marinade

2 tablespoons salt-reduced soy sauce

¼ cup mirin (rice wine) or dry sherry

1 tablespoon rice vinegar

1 tablespoon brown sugar

2 teaspoons grated ginger

Salad

250g soba noodles

1 tablespoon rice wine vinegar

2 tablespoons olive oil

few drops sesame oil

1 tablespoon salt-reduced soy sauce

2 teaspoons lime or lemon juice

1 tablespoon sesame seeds

2 tablespoons finely sliced pickled ginger

1 green onion, finely chopped

1 red capsicum, cut into thin strips

2 stalks crisp celery, finely sliced

Chill the beef in the freezer until firm, then slice horizontally into thin slices. Combine the marinade ingredients and pour over the beef. Cover and refrigerate for 1 hour. Alternatively, you can marinate the whole fillet, sear the outside quickly, then slice thinly.

Cook the noodles according to directions on packet, then plunge into iced water to cool. Drain well. Whisk together the vinegar, oils, soy and juice. Toast the sesame seeds in a pan until brown and add the dressing. Place the noodles in a bowl and toss through the dressing and vegetables.

Remove meat from marinade and pat dry. Heat a non-stick frying pan to very hot, brush with oil, add the meat and sear for 10–20 seconds on each side, brushing continually with marinade. Serve immediately on the noodle salad.

Slow-roast Beef in Red Wine with Potato Gnocchi

Serves 6

2205 kilojoules/**525** calories per serve; **7.5g** total fat; **1.9g** saturated fat; **585mg** sodium

A salad and bread for scooping up the leftovers are ideal accompaniments to this dish.

700g lean round or sirloin steak, trimmed

¼ cup plain flour

2 teaspoons dried thyme or oregano

pepper to taste

2 carrots, sliced

1 parsnip, sliced

2 cups mushrooms, quartered

1 onion, sliced

250ml (1 cup) red wine

250ml (1 cup) beef or chicken stock

½ cup water

potato gnocchi (see note)

About gnocchi

Always check the label on gnocchi packets. Avoid the ones with high-fat cheeses, butter and cream near the start of the ingredients. A bit of butter and parmesan right at the end of the list is all right, but the best gnocchi is straight potato, flour, eggs and seasonings.

Preheat oven to 170°C.

Cut the meat into large cubes, removing excess fat. Place in a plastic bag with the flour, thyme and pepper and shake well to coat meat. Place in a large casserole with the vegetables and toss to combine. Pour over the wine, stock and water and bake for 2½–3 hours or until meat is tender. Halfway through cooking, give the casserole a stir to circulate ingredients. Bring a large pot of water to the boil, add gnocchi and cook until they rise to the surface – about 10 minutes, or according to instructions. Serve the beef and vegetables over the gnocchi in warmed large bowls to hold the juices.

Soy and Ginger Braised Chicken (page 78)

poultry

Soy and Ginger Braised Chicken

Serves 4

1770 kilojoules/**425** calories per serve; **10g** total fat; **1.9g** saturated fat; **550mg** sodium

Snow peas, baby corn, carrots and broccoli are good vegetables to use.

4 chicken maryland (about 1kg) or 1 small chicken cut into quarters
1 tablespoon peanut or olive oil
1 tablespoon grated ginger
¾ cup chicken stock
¼ cup sherry
2 tablespoons salt-reduced soy sauce
1 tablespoon lemon juice
1 tablespoon honey or brown sugar
3 cups mixed Asian vegetables, cut into strips (see note)
2 cups hot steamed rice

Remove all the skin and fat from chicken.

Heat the oil in a heavy-based frying pan, add the ginger and cook for 1–2 minutes. Add the chicken and brown all over. Turn the chicken flesh side up and pour in the stock, sherry, soy sauce, lemon juice and honey. Cover tightly, reduce heat and braise for 45–50 minutes or until very tender and cooked through. Spoon over liquid during cooking to keep the flesh moist. Remove chicken and keep warm. Skim any fat from the surface of the liquid and boil for 5–6 minutes to thin sauce consistency.

In a separate wok or pan, stir-fry the vegetables until tender but still crisp.

To serve, you can either leave the chicken on the bone, or remove and shred the flesh. Serve on the rice with some of the sauce spooned over and the vegetables on the side.

Chinese Chicken Noodle Pancakes

Makes 4 pancakes

1230 kilojoules/**295** calories per serve; **9g** total fat; **2.3g** saturated fat; **325mg** sodium

45g packet fine noodles such as vermicelli or cellophane
3 eggs
¼ cup plain flour
200g cooked chicken breast, cut into thin slivers
½ cup corn kernels
¼ cup snipped chives or green onions
¼ cup chopped fresh coriander
2 teaspoons salt-reduced soy or oyster sauce
peanut or olive oil for brushing pan

Glaze
2 tablespoons plum sauce
2 teaspoons salt reduced soy sauce
¼ cup sherry or rice wine

Combine the glaze ingredients in a small saucepan and bring to the boil. Reduce heat and keep warm.

Soak the noodles in boiling water for 5 minutes or until soft, drain well, cool and chop into small pieces. In a large bowl, beat the eggs then fold in the flour, followed by the noodles, chicken, corn, herbs and soy sauce.

Heat a non stick pan to high and brush with oil. Pour in ¼ of the mixture and cook until browned underneath and set on top. Turn and brush with the glaze. Cook until browned underneath. Transfer to a plate and keep warm in a low oven while remainder are cooked. Serve hot with leftover glaze spooned over.

Chinese Chicken Noodle Pancakes

Olive, Basil and Cheese-filled Chicken Breast

Serves 4

1435 kilojoules/**345** calories per serve; **15g** total fat; **4.1g** saturated fat; **345mg** sodium

Serve with crusty Italian or sourdough bread.

To stone olives, simply place them on a wooden board, place a broad knife, such as a cook's knife or a cleaver on top and press with the flat of your hand. This will split the olive and you can remove the stone. No fancy equipment needed! Stoned olives are available in jars, but the convenience does not make up for the loss of flavour. Olives are best bought in Middle Eastern or Italian delis, where you can sample the many different varieties before buying.

4 chicken breast fillets, about 130g–150g each
¼ cup stoned black olives
2 teaspoons olive oil
juice of 1 lemon
1 clove garlic, crushed, optional
freshly ground black pepper to taste
8 large basil leaves
2 bocconcini, sliced
250ml (1 cup) dry white wine
1 bunch rocket
4 roma or vine-ripened tomatoes, thickly
  sliced

Dressing
2 tablespoons balsamic vinegar
1 tablespoon olive oil

Preheat oven to 180°C.

Flatten the chicken breasts between two sheets of baking paper, or ask your butcher to flatten them for you. Combine the olives, olive oil, 2 teaspoons of the lemon juice and garlic in a food processor until coarsely ground. You could also finely chop the olives and mash with the oil and lemon, if preferred. Season to taste with pepper.

Lay chicken breasts on a board with the inside facing up and spread with the olive paste. Lay 2 leaves of basil down one side of each breast and top with slices of bocconcini, leaving a border at each end. Tuck in the ends and roll up. Secure with skewers or tie with string and place side by side in a casserole dish. Pour in the wine and remaining lemon juice. Some extra basil or coriander leaves will add to the flavour.

Cover loosely with foil and bake for 30 minutes or until just cooked and the juices run clear when pierced with a knife. Remove foil, brush with a little olive oil and return to the oven for 5 minutes to crisp the surface. Remove from casserole dish, cover and allow to sit for 5 minutes.

Arrange rocket leaves and tomatoes on plates and drizzle with the dressing. Slice each breast in 3–4 large slices and arrange over the salad.

Marinated Chicken and Mung Bean Salad

Serves 4

1140 kilojoules/**270** calories per serve; **9g** total fat; **1.8g** saturated fat; **330mg** sodium

Serve this cold or as a hot salad, the choice is yours.

500g chicken breast or thigh fillets, cut into strips
1 teaspoon sesame oil
2 tablespoons hoisin sauce
¼ cup sherry or red wine
1 tablespoon grated ginger
1 tablespoon sesame seeds
2 teaspoons peanut or olive oil

Salad

1 cup mung bean or bean sprouts
1 cup shredded red cabbage
1 red capsicum, finely sliced
12 snow peas, blanched and cut into strips
2 tablespoons rice wine vinegar
1 teaspoon fish sauce, optional

Combine the chicken, sesame oil, hoisin, sherry, ginger and sesame seeds and marinate at least 2 hours or overnight. Heat a wok or non-stick pan to high and add the peanut oil. When hot, add the chicken and stir-fry for 4–5 minutes or until cooked. Transfer to a shallow pan and chill.

Combine the salad ingredients and toss with the combined vinegar and fish sauce. Serve the chicken scattered over the salad, with a bowl of rice or noodles on the side.

Balsamic-marinated Chicken with Lemon Couscous

Serves 4

1385 kilojoules/**330** calories per serve; **5.5g** total fat; **1.6g** saturated fat; **120mg** sodium

4 chicken breasts fillets, about 600g, flattened
¼ cup balsamic vinegar
¼ cup apple juice
1 red capsicum, roasted, seeded and peeled
freshly ground pepper to taste

Lemon Couscous

2 cups chicken stock
1 cup couscous
1 tablespoon chopped fresh coriander
1 tablespoon chopped fresh Italian parsley
1 green onion, finely sliced
grated zest and juice of 1 lemon
1 teaspoon olive oil

Trim the chicken fillets and place in a deep-sided ceramic dish. Pour over the balsamic vinegar and 2 tablespoons of the apple juice, cover, and marinate overnight. Puree the capsicum in a food processor or blender with the remaining apple juice and a little wine or stock if too dry. Season to taste with pepper and set aside.

To make the Lemon Couscous, bring the stock to the boil, add the couscous, herbs and onion, cover and turn the heat off. Allow to steam for 10 minutes or until all liquid is absorbed. Fluff with a fork, while adding the zest, juice and oil, and season to taste with pepper. Keep warm.

Drain the marinade from the chicken and grill or barbecue until cooked through, brushing with the marinade during cooking. Serve over the couscous with a spoon of the red capsicum purée.

Lemon Turkey Burgers with Herb Mayonnaise

Makes 4 large burgers (Note: high in salt, reduce the amount of Worcestershire sauce, if desired)

1995 kilojoules/**475** calories per serve; **11g** total fat; **2.5g** saturated fat; **1215mg** sodium

If you can't buy minced turkey, simply buy fillets, remove the skin and chop finely before putting in the food processor. Or use chicken instead.

Gathering the herbs for a herb mayonnaise can be as easy as stepping out of your kitchen door or snipping away on your window sill. Planted in a sunny position, herbs will flourish even through the winter and whether you have acres of soil or just a few pots on a balcony, the delights of homegrown fresh produce can be yours to reap.

1 small onion, finely chopped

500g lean minced turkey (see note)

2 teaspoons grated lemon rind

1 teaspoon thyme leaves

½ cup fresh grated breadcrumbs

1 tablespoon salt-reduced
   Worcestershire sauce

olive oil and lemon juice for brushing burgers

4 thick gourmet buns, such as rye, sourdough,
   grain, or thickly sliced bread

curly lettuce leaves

thickly sliced tomato and cucumber

Herb Mayonnaise

¼ cup each chopped parsley and
   coriander, or mint

1 tablespoon chopped dill

1 green onion, chopped

1 tablespoons low-fat mayonnaise

¼ cup low-fat natural yoghurt

2 teaspoons lemon juice

cracked pepper to taste

To make the Herb Mayonnaise, place the fresh herbs and green onion in a food processor or pass through a mill to make a coarse paste. Place in a small bowl with the mayonnaise, yoghurt, lemon juice and pepper and mix well. Cover and chill at least 10 minutes to allow flavours to develop.

Combine onion, turkey, rind, thyme, breadcrumbs and Worcestershire sauce in a food processor and process until well mixed, or mix with hands in a large bowl. Shape into four burgers and barbecue or grill on a preheated grill pan for 5–6 minutes on each side, or until cooked through and no longer pink inside. Brush with olive oil and lemon juice during cooking.

Split bread in half and place on grill at end of cooking to warm. Arrange curly lettuce leaves, thickly sliced tomato and cucumber on bottom half of roll, top with turkey burgers and a spoon on the herb mayonnaise.

Warm Chicken and Apple Salad

Serves 6

1095 kilojoules/**260** calories per serve; **11g** total fat; **1.4g** saturated fat; **130mg** sodium

This salad is great served with a baguette or rye bread.

½ cup raisins

2 tablespoons port or red wine

½ cup apple juice

400g diced skinless chicken

2 green apples, diced

2 teaspoons each grated lemon rind and juice

2 stalks celery, chopped

½ cup walnut halves, roasted

1 bunch cos or mixed lettuce

Dressing

2 tablespoons low-fat natural yoghurt

2 tablespoons low-fat mayonnaise

Place the raisins, port and apple juice in a large saucepan and bring to the boil. Reduce heat, add the chicken, cover and simmer for 10–15 minutes or until chicken is cooked. Drain and discard liquid.

Place the apples, lemon rind and juice, celery and walnuts in a bowl and toss to combine. Combine the yoghurt and mayonnaise and toss through the salad. Arrange lettuce in a bowl or on plates, top with the salad and spoon over the chicken and raisins.

Hot Chicken Caesar Baguettes with Avocado Dressing

Serves 2

2550 kilojoules/**610** calories per serve; **29g** total fat; **6.9g** saturated fat; **840mg** sodium

200g chicken breast fillet

3 teaspoons extra virgin olive oil

ground black pepper

2 pieces baguette, about 20cm each

2 large cos lettuce leaves

2 cooked free-range eggs, quartered

2 teaspoons shredded parmesan cheese

Dressing

½ avocado, chopped

2 anchovies, drained and rinsed

1 tablespoon low-fat yoghurt

1 tablespoon lemon juice

1 teaspoon salt-reduced Worcestershire sauce

Beat together the dressing ingredients until smooth and set aside.

Brush the chicken with 1 teaspoon of the oil, season to taste with pepper and char-grill or grill until cooked through. Split the baguettes in half lengthwise and brush with the remaining oil. Lay open on an oven tray and bake or grill until crisp and hot. Place a lettuce leaf on each baguette, top with the chicken and egg and spoon over some dressing. Sprinkle with the parmesan, close the baguette and eat while hot.

Penne with Char-grilled Chicken and Eggplant

Serves 4

2840 kilojoules/**680** calories per serve; **12g** total fat; **3g** saturated fat; **275mg** sodium

When choosing pasta to match a hearty, chunky sauce, select short, chunky shapes, such as penne, rigatoni, pipe, conchiglie, casareccia, gnocchi, fusilli, elicoidali and maccheroni. When choosing pasta to match a thin, creamy, clingy sauce, select long shapes, such as spaghetti, spaghettini, vermicelli, capellini, fedelini, linguine, fettuccine, trenette and tagliolini.

500g penne pasta

1 tablespoon extra virgin olive oil

500g chicken breast or thigh fillets

4 thick slices eggplant

1 clove garlic, crushed

2 green onions, sliced

2 tablespoons semi-dried tomatoes, sliced

2 roma tomatoes, seeded and diced

2 teaspoons fresh oregano leaves

¼ cup chicken stock

¼ cup dry white wine

2 cups sliced rocket or baby spinach leaves

¼ cup reduced-fat fetta cheese, rinsed and crumbled

Cook the pasta according to directions, drain well, toss with a teaspoon of the oil and keep warm. Brush the chicken and eggplant with oil and season to taste with pepper. Char-grill both in a preheated grill pan or heavy-based frying pan for 1–2 minutes on each side or until the chicken is browned but not cooked right through and the eggplant is brown and soft. Remove from pan and set aside.

Heat the remaining oil in a large frying pan and sauté the garlic and green onions for 1–2 minutes or until soft. Add both the tomatoes and oregano and cook for 2–3 minutes. Add the stock and wine and bring to the boil. Slice the chicken thickly and add to the pan.

Cover, reduce the heat and cook for 5–6 minutes or until chicken is cooked. Add the rocket and cook for 1 minute, then toss through the pasta and heat through. Serve topped with the crumbled fetta.

Turkey and Garden Vegetable Terrine with Oregano and Thyme

Serves 6 – a 27cm loaf (about 18 thick slices)

805 kilojoules/**190** calories per serve; **10g** total fat; **1.9g** saturated fat; **240mg** sodium

Serve cold or reheated, with salad and bread, or sliced on a sandwich.

Turkey meat is a good source of iron and protein and is low in fat.

Terrine is not only the name of the finished dish but also the vessel it is cooked in, originally an earthenware, ovenproof dish.

1–2 tablespoons white wine

2 green onions, chopped

1 cup sliced mushrooms

500g minced turkey or chicken breast (or finely chopped skinless breast and thigh meat)

1 egg

½ cup low-fat milk

1 tablespoon each fresh oregano and thyme leaves or 1 teaspoon each dried

2 tablespoons chopped fresh parsley or basil

pepper, to taste

1 carrot, diced

1 zucchini, diced

½ cup chopped pistachio nuts

3–4 large spinach or large butter lettuce leaves, lightly blanched

Preheat oven to 175°C. Line a 10cm x 27cm loaf tin with plastic wrap, leaving an overhang to cover the top of the terrine.

Heat the wine and cook the onions and mushrooms until soft. Cool. Place the turkey and egg in a food processor and process to a fine paste. Add the milk and herbs, season with pepper, and pulse on and off until ingredients are just incorporated. Cover and refrigerate. Lightly blanch or steam the carrot and zucchini until just tender. Drain and pat dry with kitchen paper.

Fold all the vegetables and nuts through the mince. Line the prepared loaf tin with the spinach leaves. Spoon in mixture and press down well. Top with spinach and enclose with plastic over top. Cover with foil. Place in a large deep-sided baking dish and pour in enough boiling water to come ⅔ of the way up the sides. Bake for 1 hour or until juices run clear when tested with a skewer or sharp knife.

Remove foil and plastic from top and cool to room temperature on a wire rack. Unmould on a tray to allow juices to escape. Return to clean loaf tin, cover and refrigerate overnight.

Chicken, Macadamia and Noodle Stir-fry

Serves 4

2730 kilojoules/**650** calories per serve; **23g** total fat; **3.6g** saturated fat; **630mg** sodium

These noodles can be found in Asian food stores and most supermarkets.

500g skinless, boneless chicken breast, sliced

¼ cup dry sherry or rice wine

2 tablespoons oyster sauce

1 tablespoon salt-reduced soy sauce

2 teaspoons cornflour

400g packet rice stick or soba noodles (see note)

½ cup raw whole and half macadamias

1 tablespoon peanut or macadamia oil

1 knob ginger, sliced

2 green onions, chopped

1 red capsicum, sliced

2 cups chopped asparagus or green beans

70–100ml (about ⅓–½ cup) chicken stock

Place chicken in a bowl and stir through the sherry, sauces and cornflour. Cover and marinate in the refrigerator for at least 30 minutes. Cover noodles with boiling water and soak 10–15 minutes to soften. Drain.

Heat a wok and stir-fry macadamias until golden. Remove from pan, add half the oil and stir-fry ginger 1 minute, add vegetables and stir-fry 2 minutes. Set aside. Add remaining oil, remove chicken from marinade and stir-fry 3–5 minutes or until just cooked. Add vegetables, 70ml of the stock and noodles and toss together until heated through, adding more stock if necessary. Add macadamias just before serving.

Lemon and Almond-crusted Chicken on Sweet Potato Mash

Serves 4

1390 kilojoules/**330** calories per serve; **13g** total fat; **2.5g** saturated fat; **150mg** sodium

Serve with a big green side salad or steamed greens.

1 tablespoon extra virgin olive oil

1 tablespoon lemon juice

4 chicken breast or thigh fillets, about 130–150g each

2 tablespoons grated lemon zest

2 tablespoons finely chopped or ground almonds

2 teaspoons grated parmesan cheese

125–250ml (½–1 cup) chicken stock

Sweet Potato Mash

400g piece sweet potato, peeled and diced

¼ cup buttermilk or low-fat milk

cracked black pepper to taste

Preheat the oven to 180°C.

Combine the oil and 1 teaspoon of the lemon juice and brush over the chicken fillets. Pan-fry in a non-stick pan for 1–2 minutes each side to brown the surface. Transfer the fillets to an ovenproof dish. Combine the remaining juice, lemon zest, almonds and parmesan cheese and press over the top of the chicken. Pour in enough chicken stock to come to about 1cm up dish. Bake for 30–40 minutes or until cooked through.

Meanwhile, cook the sweet potato until tender, mash and stir in the buttermilk and pepper to taste. Reheat and serve topped with the chicken.

Satay-crusted Chicken and Basmati Pilau

Serves 4

2165 kilojoules/**515** calories per serve; **11g** total fat; **2g** saturated fat; **155mg** sodium

Check the label on peanut butters. Unnecessary added fats, sugar and salt often replace the wonderful natural oils and nutrient of the peanuts. Try a freshly ground one from a health food store. Just buy a small amount and keep in the fridge.

Basmati rice is frequently chosen for pilau because of its long grain, giving the dish a fluffy result, while the grains remain separate and firm. Basmati also has a deliciously fragrant flavour.

4 chicken breast fillets, about 125g each
⅓ cup roasted unsalted peanuts or ¼ cup
   crunchy roasted peanut butter (see note)
1 red chilli, chopped or 1 teaspoon chilli sauce
2 teaspoons salt-reduced soy sauce
2 teaspoons lemon juice
1 clove garlic, crushed
lemon wedges and a salad, to serve

Pilau
1 white onion, diced
2 teaspoons olive oil
1½ cups basmati rice
750ml (3 cups) water
1 bay leaf
1 teaspoon fresh thyme leaves
½ cup chopped green beans
1 tablespoon chopped flat-leaf parsley

Cut each fillet into 3 long strips. In a food processor, combine the peanuts, chilli, soy, lemon juice and garlic. Purée to a coarse paste, so there are still some chunks of nuts. Add a little water if mixture is too coarse. Spread over the chicken, cover and refrigerate for 1 hour.

In a large saucepan, sauté the onion in the oil until soft. Add the rice and sauté for 1 minute. Add the water, bay leaf and thyme and bring to the boil. Reduce the heat to low, cover, and simmer for 20 minutes. Add the beans and parsley and cook 5–7 minutes or until rice is tender and liquid is absorbed. If your saucepan doesn't have a very tight seal, you may need to add more water during cooking.

While the rice is cooking, place the chicken on a foil-lined grill and cook under a medium heat for 5–6 minutes each side or until cooked through. Serve with the hot rice, lemon wedges and a salad.

Mediterranean Chicken Strudel

Makes 4 strudels

1450 kilojoules/**345** calories per serve; **12g** total fat; **3.3g** saturated fat; **360mg** sodium

Serve as a meal
with a large side
salad and bread or
just enjoy as
a snack.

1 large red capsicum

4 spinach leaves

4 chicken breast fillets, about 150g each

olive oil and fresh lemon juice, for brushing

⅓ cup fresh low-fat ricotta cheese

2 teaspoons grated lemon rind

freshly ground pepper to taste

8 sheets filo pastry

1 tablespoon grated parmesan cheese

Preheat oven to 180°C.

Cut the capsicum in quarters, remove seeds and grill or roast, skin side up until skin blackens. Seal in a bag for 10 minutes, then peel. Blanch or steam the spinach leaves until just starting to soften. Pat dry and set aside.

Flatten chicken breast fillets to about 1cm thickness or cut fillet horizontally and fold out like a butterfly. Brush with a little olive oil and lemon. Spread ricotta over one side of the fillet and season with lemon rind and pepper. Top with a slice of the roasted red capsicum.

Fold one half of the chicken over the other and wrap in a spinach leaf.

Lay 2 sheets of filo pastry on a dry board, brush with oil and season with pepper. Place chicken parcel on one end, fold in the ends and wrap up like a parcel. Brush top with oil,

Sprinkle with parmesan and bake on a lightly oiled or lined oven tray for 25–30 minutes or until chicken is cooked.

Thai Chicken Curry with Papaya Raita

Serves 4

1510 kilojoules/**360** calories per serve; **9g** total fat; **3g** saturated fat; **180mg** sodium

Using water
makes a lighter,
fresher curry. For
a creamier, richer
texture, use
evaporated
skim milk.

2 teaspoons extra virgin olive oil

1 clove garlic, crushed

2 spring onions, chopped

1 stalk lemongrass, white part only, chopped

1 tablespoon green curry paste, or to taste

450g–500g chicken breast fillet, sliced

200ml water (see note)

175ml light coconut milk

1 kaffir lime leaf

1 red capsicum, finely diced

1 cucumber, seeded and diced

2 cups steamed Thai jasmine rice, to serve

Papaya Raita

1 cup finely diced papaya

juice of 1 lime

½ lebanese cucumber, grated

¼ cup low-fat yoghurt

Heat the oil in a large saucepan. Add the garlic, onion and lemongrass and cook until soft. Add the curry paste and chicken and cook until chicken is browned. Add the water, coconut milk and lime leaf and bring to the boil. Cook for 20 minutes then add the capsicum and cucumber. Cook for 20 minutes or until chicken is tender and sauce is thick and fragrant.

While the chicken is cooking combine the raita ingredients in a bowl and mix well. Set aside until ready to serve. Remove leaf from curry and serve with rice and the Papaya Raita.

Caprese Pide Pizza (page 100)

no meat

Caprese Pide Pizza

Makes 4 'pizzas'

2035 kilojoules/**485** calories per serve; **24g** total fat; **9.6g** saturated fat; **680mg** sodium

Slice the tops of the pide thinly and bake until crisp, to use with dips or just to munch on.

4 round pide breads or 1 long loaf
   (Turkish bread)
2 tablespoons olive oil
1 clove garlic, cut in half
4 roma tomatoes, sliced
16 large fresh basil leaves
4 bocconcini, about 50g–60g each, sliced
cracked black pepper to taste
1 tablespoon capers, rinsed (optional)

Preheat oven to 190°C.

Slice a thin layer from the top of the pide, so the fillings will sit evenly (see note). Brush the pide with oil and rub with the garlic. Arrange tomato, basil and bocconcini on the bread. Season to taste with pepper and scatter with capers, if used. Bake for 10–15 minutes or until cheese is golden and base is crisp, then place under a grill for 2 minutes, or until the cheese browns. Serve straight from the oven.

Char-grilled Vegetable Salad with Dill Cheese Dressing

Serves 4

685 kilojoules/**165** calories per serve; **12g** total fat; **2.4g** saturated fat; **130mg** sodium

Serve with lemon wedges and thickly sliced bread or a bowl of pasta to toss through. It is also nice sitting on a bed of lettuce.

2 tablespoons olive oil
3 tablespoons lime or lemon juice
¼ cup crumbled fat-reduced goat or
   fetta cheese
1 tablespoon dill leaves
2 small zucchini, cut into 3 lengthwise
2 red capsicum, seeded, halved and
   pressed flat
2 witlof (Belgian endive), halved lengthwise
cracked pepper to taste
8 large flat mushrooms

Heat a grill pan or barbecue to high. Combine the oil and lemon juice and purée half in a food processor with the cheese to a smooth paste. Alternatively, mash all together with a fork in a small bowl. Stir in the dill and set aside. Cook the zucchini, capsicum and witlof on the hot grill for 5–6 minutes, turning and brushing with the remaining oil and juice or until tender and slightly browned. Season to taste with pepper. Add the mushrooms half way through cooking and grill until juices start to escape. Serve vegetables with a spoonful of the dressing.

Char-grilled Vegetable Salad with Dill Cheese Dressing

Spicy Noodle and Peanut Sang Choy Bow

Makes 6

620 kilojoules/**150** calories per serve; **4.5g** total fat; **0.6g** saturated fat; **150mg** sodium

200g hokkien or soba noodles

few drops sesame oil

1 tablespoon salt-reduced soy sauce

2 teaspoons plum or oyster sauce

¼ cup roasted peanuts, roughly chopped

1 cup bean sprouts

½ cup shredded carrot

1 green onion, chopped

2 tablespoons chopped fresh coriander

6 firm large lettuce leaves, such as
  radicchio or butter lettuce

Cook the noodles according to directions and drain well. Place in a bowl and toss with the oil and sauces. Add the peanuts, sprouts, carrot, green onion and coriander, and toss to combine. Spoon mixture into lettuce cups and serve straight away.

Lemon Vegetable Pilaf

Serves 4

2075 kilojoules/**495** calories per serve; **12g** total fat; **1.2g** saturated fat; **50mg** sodium

1 tablespoon olive oil

⅓ cup slivered almonds

¼ cup chopped dried apricots

¼ cup sliced dates

1 teaspoon ground cinnamon

1 onion, chopped

1½ cups basmati rice

2 teaspoons ground cumin

pinch saffron

1 teaspoon allspice

375ml (1½ cups) vegetable stock

½ cup white wine

juice and grated zest of 1 lemon

1 cup cauliflower florets

1 cup broccoli florets

1 cup peas

Heat 2 teaspoons of the oil in a large saucepan. Add the almonds, apricots, sultanas, dates and cinnamon and cook, stirring until nuts are golden brown. Remove from the pan, drain on absorbent paper and set aside.

Add the remaining 2 teaspoons oil and the onion to the pan and cook until onions are soft. Add the rice, cumin, saffron and allspice to the pan and cook, stirring for 1–2 minutes. Pour in the stock, wine and lemon and bring to the boil. Reduce heat to low, add the cauliflower, cover with a tight-fitting lid and cook for 15 minutes.

Add the remaining vegetables and a little more water or stock if mixture is dry. Cover and cook for a further 5–7 minutes or until the rice is cooked and vegetables are tender. Serve scattered with the reserved almond fruit mixture.

Asparagus and Pine Nut Tarts

Makes 6 regular muffin-sized tarts

1385 kilojoules/**330** calories per serve; **19g** total fat; **3.4g** saturated fat; **80mg** sodium

Ricotta has a high moisture content and in some cases draining it in a lined colander may be necessary. Best eaten on the day you've bought it, ricotta has a fresh, light flavour and makes a light dessert, with fruit or nuts, or simply drizzled with a little honey, or dusted with cocoa powder.

Pine nuts have a high oil content – 81 per cent unsaturated (equally mono and polyunsaturated), good protein and iron, and a sweet flavour. Keep refrigerated, because rancidity can be a problem. Roasting improves the flavour.

Pastry

½ cup pine nuts
1½ cups flour
2 tablespoons olive oil
½ cup low-fat milk
1 teaspoon grated lemon rind

Filling

8–10 spears fresh asparagus
¾ cup fresh low-fat ricotta cheese
¼ cup low-fat yoghurt
1–2 tablespoons chopped fresh dill
cracked pepper to taste
2 tablespoons pine nuts, extra

To make pastry, place pine nuts in a food processor and process for 30 seconds or until they have started to break up. Add the flour and process until combined. Combine the oil, milk and lemon rind, and gradually pour in with the motor running until the mixture clumps and forms a dough. Transfer to a well-floured board and knead until smooth. Wrap in plastic and refrigerate for 30 minutes.

Preheat oven to 180°C.

Roll out pastry and cut to fit six muffin or tart tins. Gently ease into lightly oiled tins and prick base evenly with a fork. Bake for 15 minutes then allow to cool for 10 minutes.

Plunge the asparagus into boiling water, cook for 30 seconds then run under cold water to stop cooking. Pat dry with a paper towel and cut into 3cm lengths. Beat together the ricotta, yoghurt and dill and season to taste with pepper. Spoon mixture into tarts and top with asparagus and pine nuts. Return to the oven and bake for 8–10 minutes or until the filling has set. Serve the tarts hot or cold.

Roast Fennel, Carrot and Walnut Salad

Serves 6

660 kilojoules/**160** calories per serve; **12g** total fat; **1.3g** saturated fat; **80mg** sodium

Enjoy with some crusty, hot sourdough or wood-fired bread and fresh ricotta cheese.

2 fennel bulbs

4 carrots

2 tablespoons olive oil

50g walnut halves and pieces

6–8 basil leaves, torn

2 tablespoons red wine vinegar

1 tablespoon lemon juice

baby spinach, to serve

Preheat oven to 180°C.

Remove any tough outer stalks and the green leaves from the fennel. Cut each into 6–8 wedges from top to bottom. Peel the carrots and cut each into 4 wedges. Brush the fennel and carrot with 1 tablespoon of the oil and place on an oiled oven tray or casserole dish. Bake for 30 minutes or until nearly tender. Add the walnuts and basil and cook for 5 minutes or until walnuts are crisp and aromatic.

Whisk the remaining oil, vinegar and juice together. Serve the roast vegetables and walnuts on a bed of baby spinach leaves. Spoon over the dressing.

Pumpkin and Cannellini Toasted Sandwiches

Makes 4

760 kilojoules/**180** calories per serve; **3g** total fat; **1g** saturated fat; **510mg** sodium

These toasted sandwiches are delicious with a mixture of tomato sauce and yoghurt for an easy Sunday night snack.

1 cup grated pumpkin

⅓ cup canned, drained cannellini or white beans

2 tablespoons chopped fresh coriander

½ teaspoon ground cumin

8 slices bread

2 tablespoons grain mustard

2 tablespoons low-fat fresh ricotta

Combine the pumpkin, beans, coriander and cumin in a small bowl and mix well. Spread bread with mustard on one side, ricotta on the other, and place a spoonful of the mixture in the centre of each sandwich. Cook in a sandwich or jaffle-maker or just toast under a grill.

Potato, Chickpea and Cashew Curry

Serves 6

1090 kilojoules/**260** calories per serve; **11g** total fat; **1.8g** saturated fat; **275mg** sodium

When cooking curries, spices are often the most important flavouring. Buy spices whole, never ground – these lose their flavour very quickly once the jar is opened

To roast spices, place them in a dry frying pan and set over moderate heat. Shake the pan from time to time and roast until you can smell their particular aroma, and little wafts of smoke start to escape. This will take only a few minutes. Don't burn them, as they will become bitter. Use a mortar or clean coffee grinder to grind the spices.

1 tablespoon olive oil
1 tablespoon mustard seeds
1 teaspoon coriander seeds
1 teaspoon cumin seeds
1 tablespoon chopped ginger
1 large onion, chopped
1 tablespoon curry paste (mild or hot, to taste)
400g potatoes, peeled and diced
400g can chickpeas, drained and well rinsed
400g can diced tomatoes, no added salt
½ cup vegetable stock or water
½ cup dry-roasted cashews
250g green beans

Cucumber Raita

1 cup natural low-fat yoghurt
1 lebanese cucumber, grated
2 tablespoons chopped mint
2 tablespoons lemon juice

Heat oil in a large, heavy-based saucepan and cook the mustard, coriander and cumin seeds until they start to pop. Add the ginger, onion and curry paste and cook for 2–3 minutes or until onion is soft. Add the potato, chickpeas, tomatoes and stock and bring to the boil. Reduce heat, cover and simmer for 20–30 minutes, or until potato is tender, adding more water if necessary. Stir in the cashews.

Meanwhile combine the Cucumber Raita ingredients and refrigerate until ready to serve.

Steam or blanch the beans until just tender. Keep warm.

Serve curry surrounded by the beans and with the Cucumber Raita separately.

Risoni with Roast Vegetables and Almond Pesto

Serves 4

2830 kilojoules/**675** calories per serve; **22g** total fat; **3g** saturated fat; **50mg** sodium

A splash of balsamic or red wine vinegar and a grind of pepper give this dish an added lift, and some Italian bread is great for soaking up any leftover pesto.

1 cup diced pumpkin

3 small zucchini, chopped

olive oil, to brush

ground black pepper

herbs of choice

1 large red capsicum, halved and seeded

1 bunch asparagus, each spear cut
 into 3 even lengths

12 cherry tomatoes, halved

500g risoni pasta

Almond Pesto

50g dry-roasted almonds

1 cup chopped fresh basil

½ cup chopped fresh coriander or parsley

1 tablespoon lemon juice

2 tablespoons extra virgin olive oil

1 tablespoon grated parmesan cheese

Preheat the oven to 180°C.

Place the pumpkin and zucchini on a lined baking tray, brush with olive oil and season to taste with pepper or herbs of choice. Roast for 20 minutes or until the pumpkin is tender. Add the capsicum, asparagus and tomatoes, cut side up, after 10 minutes of cooking. Remove from the oven, allow to cool slightly, then peel the capsicum and cut into 1cm slices.

While the vegetables are roasting, cook the risoni according to directions on packet. Drain and keep warm.

Place the pesto ingredients in a food processor and process to a coarse paste, adding a little stock or vinegar if mixture is too thick for your taste. Toss a tablespoon of the pesto through the hot risone. Serve topped with the roasted vegetables and remaining pesto.

Spinach, Mushroom and Tofu Lasagne

Serves 2 as a light meal

1165 kilojoules/**280** calories per serve; **22g** total fat; **3g** saturated fat; **340mg** sodium

300g block fresh firm silken tofu

8 oyster mushrooms

1 tablespoon extra virgin olive oil

1 tablespoon rice wine vinegar

1 tablespoon salt-reduced soy sauce

few drops sesame oil

2 cups baby spinach leaves, cut into
 long thin strips

1 tablespoon sesame seeds, plus
 2 teaspoons extra

Drain tofu well and cover with kitchen paper. Place on a plate and refrigerate for 20 minutes. Lightly sauté or grill oyster mushrooms until just starting to soften and lose moisture. Set aside. Whisk together the oil, vinegar, soy sauce and sesame oil. Slice the block of tofu in half horizontally, then slice each piece in half, so each portion has 2 pieces of tofu.

Just before serving, toast the sesame seeds and toss one tablespoon through the dressing – they should sizzle as the hot hits the cold and the flavours infuse.

To serve, place one slice of tofu on a plate, top with a mushroom then some of the spinach. Repeat, drizzle with the dressing and sprinkle with the remaining sesame seeds. Serve immediately.

Potato Burgers with Roast Tomato Relish

Makes about 6 burgers

770 kilojoules/**185** calories per serve (without bread rolls); **5.5g** total fat; **1g** saturated fat; **40mg** sodium

The relish can be stored in the refrigerator for a few days in a sealed container, or served hot with the burgers. Serve the burgers on rocket leaves or bread rolls with salad and the relish.

Roasting tomatoes brings out their flavour, particularly during winter, when these – essentially summer – fruits are not at their best. The addition of balsamic vinegar and fresh basil ensure a lively relish, no matter what time of year.

3 large potatoes, peeled and diced – try sebago, bintje or coliban
½ cup sliced leek
½ red capsicum, raw or roasted and chopped
1 teaspoon thyme leaves
2 tablespoons fresh parsley
2 eggs, lightly beaten
pepper-seasoned flour, for coating
1 tablespoon olive oil

Roast tomato relish

6 roma tomatoes, peeled and diced
1 red onion, diced
1 tablespoon brown sugar
2 tablespoons balsamic vinegar
¼ cup chopped fresh basil
cracked pepper to taste

Preheat the oven to 170°C.

To make the relish, toss all ingredients together and place in a lightly-oiled baking dish. Bake for 20 minutes or until onion is soft. Mash with a fork or blend in a food processor. Set aside (see note).

To make the burgers, cook the potatoes until just tender, adding leek about half way through cooking time. Mash and allow to cool for 10 minutes. Place in a bowl with the capsicum, thyme, parsley and eggs and mix well. Shape into burgers and coat with flour. Lay on a lined baking tray and refrigerate for 30 minutes. Heat oil in a non-stick pan and fry cakes for 5 minutes each side or until golden brown. Keep warm in a low oven while remainder are cooked. Serve immediately with the relish.

Tagliatelle with Mixed Mushroom Sauce

Serves 4

2255 kilojoules/**540** calories per serve; **6.5g** total fat; **2g** saturated fat; **80mg** sodium

A rocket and parmesan salad is an ideal accompaniment for this dish, with some sliced vine-ripened tomatoes.

20g dried porcini or other dried mushrooms

2 large field mushrooms

10 mushrooms of choice such as shitake, swiss or oyster mushrooms

2 teaspoons extra virgin olive oil

1 clove garlic, crushed

1 spring onion, sliced

¾ cup white wine

⅓ cup fresh ricotta cheese

1 tablespoon lemon juice

freshly ground pepper to taste

500g tagliatelle or fettuccine

2 tablespoons chopped flat-leaf parsley, plus extra fresh parsley or basil, to serve

Cover the dried mushrooms with boiling water and soak for 20 minutes. Drain and reserve a few tablespoons of the liquid. Thickly slice all the mushrooms. Heat the oil in a large high-sided frying pan and sauté the garlic and onion for 1 minute to soften. Add all the mushrooms and cook for 2–3 minutes or until they start to release their juices.

Add a few tablespoons of the wine to the ricotta and juice and mix together until smooth. Add to pan with the remaining wine and simmer until sauce thickens. Check for seasoning, and add pepper or extra lemon juice to taste.

Meanwhile cook the tagliatelle according to directions on the pack, strain and toss through the sauce, together with the chopped parsley. Serve sprinkled with fresh parsley or basil.

Ricotta, Pine Nut and Couscous Frittata

Serves 8

760 kilojoules/**180** calories per serve; **8.5g** total fat; **2.6g** saturated fat; **90mg** sodium

For the simplest way to peel and seed tomatoes, see the note on page 36.

2 teaspoons olive oil

1 red onion, chopped

1 zucchini, finely sliced

2 roma tomatoes, peeled, seeded (see note) and diced

2 tablespoons currants

2 teaspoons each lemon zest and juice

¼ cup chopped fresh mint

¼ cup chopped fresh parsley

1 cup cooked couscous (see directions on pack)

½ cup ricotta cheese

6 eggs

2 tablespoons pine nuts

Preheat a grill.

Heat the oil in a large non-stick frying pan (about 26–28cm). Add the onion and zucchini and cook for 2–3 minutes or until soft. Add the tomatoes, currants, zest, herbs and couscous and cook for 1–2 minutes. Beat the cheese and eggs together in a bowl, then pour over the mixture. Cook over a medium heat until the base is browned and the top is nearly set. Sprinkle with pine nuts and place under the grill until golden brown. Slice and serve hot or cold with salad.

Barley and Bean Salad

Serves 6

1350 kilojoules/**325** calories per serve; **16g** total fat; **2.4g** saturated fat; **170mg** sodium

Serve as a side or main dish over a bed of rocket or mixed lettuce.

Full of goodness, barley is one of the earliest cultivated grains, and is again gaining popularity in the western world. The most commonly used form is pearl barley – the hulled barley grain. Buy barley in healthfood shops with a good turnover and store in a cool, dark place. Barley is also used in soups and pilafs and you can use barley cooking water to make barley water, usually flavoured with lemon, lime or orange.

1 cup barley

400g can butter or haricot beans, drained and well rinsed

¼ cup chopped coriander leaves

2 tomatoes, diced

2 green onions, diced

1 cup corn kernels

1 avocado, diced

½ cup chopped string beans or celery

⅓ cup roasted hazelnuts, roughly chopped

Dressing

1 tablespoon olive or hazelnut oil

2 tablespoons red wine vinegar

1 tablespoon lemon juice

Place the barley in a large pot of boiling water and cook for 30 minutes or until tender but not soft. Drain, refresh under cold running water and allow to cool. In a large bowl combine the barley with the remaining salad ingredients.

To make the dressing, whisk together the oil, vinegar and juice and toss through the salad.

Peach and Pear Tart (page 120)

dessert

Peach and Pear Tart

Makes a 34 x 10cm rectangular tart, or a 22–23cm tart (10 slices)
770 kilojoules/**185** calories per serve; **6.5g** total fat; **1.8g** saturated fat; **75mg** sodium

½ cup ricotta cheese

2 tablespoons custard powder

½ teaspoon vanilla essence

3 canned pears, peeled and diced

3 fresh or canned, drained, peaches

apple or pear jelly for glazing (the baby food
   varieties are great for this)

Pastry

¼ cup dry-roasted almonds, chopped

2 tablespoons cornflour

1¼ cups plain flour

1 teaspoon grated lemon rind

1 tablespoon sugar

2 tablespoons margarine

80ml chilled skim milk

50ml cold water

Preheat oven to 375°C.

To make pastry, place the almonds, flours, lemon, sugar and margarine in a food processor and press the pulse button until mixture resembles breadcrumbs. With motor running, gradually pour in the milk and then water until mixture starts to clump and form a dough. Turn onto a floured board and knead gently to a smooth dough. Wrap in plastic and refrigerate 30 minutes. Roll out to fit a flan or pie dish. Gently ease into lightly oiled dish and prick evenly with a fork. Bake for 15–20 minutes or until golden brown. Transfer to a wire rack to cool. This can be made a few days ahead of time and stored in a sealed container until ready to fill.

To make filling, beat together the ricotta, custard powder, vanilla and ¼ of a pear. Spoon into tarts and top with fruit. Warm jelly in microwave for 10 seconds or over hot water until just soft and spoon over fruit.

Rum and Ricotta Tiramisu

Serves 8
915 kilojoules/**220** calories per serve; **9.5g** total fat; **5.7g** saturated fat; **200mg** sodium

For a special liqueur touch, add a tablespoon of Kahlua, Baileys Irish Cream or other coffee liqueur to the coffee.

300g low-fat ricotta cheese

200g light cream cheese

1 tablespoon rum or cognac

¼ cup caster sugar

375ml (1½ cups) very strong espresso or
   good quality coffee, cooled

16 savoiardi sponge finger biscuits
   (ladyfingers)

2 tablespoons unsweetened cocoa,
   for dusting

Beat the cheeses, rum and sugar with electric beaters until light and creamy, set aside. Pour the coffee into a large shallow dish. Quickly dip one side of half the sponge fingers into the coffee and lay closely together with the dipped side down over the base of a large flat-based serving dish. Spread half of the cheese mixture evenly over the biscuits. Dust with half the cocoa then repeat layers with coffee-dipped biscuits and cheese. Cover with plastic wrap and refrigerate for at least 6 hours or overnight. Dust with remaining cocoa just before serving.

Rum and Ricotta Tiramisu

Sauterne Cake with Berries and Crème Anglaise

Makes a 20–23cm cake (8–10 slices) and 375ml (1½) cups Crème Anglaise

1520 kilojoules/**365** calories per serve; **18g** total fat; **3.2g** saturated fat; **50mg** sodium

This cake
is equally at home
on the afternoon
tea table or as
a dessert.

Sauterne, a classic
dessert wine,
contributes
sweetness and
ensures
a moist texture.

Serve the cake
with fresh berries in
summer – at other
times of the year,
try some poached
or stewed fruit in
season, such as
plums, apples
or pears.

3 eggs, separated, plus 1 white
½ cup caster sugar
grated rind of 1 lemon
90ml extra virgin olive oil
100ml sauterne or sweet dessert wine
1¼ cups plain flour, sifted
¼ cup almond meal
berries of choice and icing sugar, to serve

Crème Anglaise
310ml (1¼) cups low-fat milk
1 vanilla bean, or 1 teaspoon vanilla essence
3 large egg yolks
⅓ cup sugar

Preheat oven to 180°C. Grease a 22–23cm springform cake tin.

To make cake, beat together the egg yolks and sugar until light and creamy. Lightly whisk in the lemon rind, oil and wine. Sift together the flour and almond meal and fold through mixture until just combined. Beat the eggwhites until stiff and fold through lightly. Spoon into prepared tin and bake for 25 minutes.

Reduce heat to 170°C and bake a further 15–20 minutes. Turn off the oven, cover cake with baking paper and allow to rest in oven for 10 minutes. The cake will sink in the centre. Remove cake from tin and cool on a wire rack or serve warm from the oven, dusted with icing sugar and scattered with berries. Spoon the Crème Anglaise around the outside.

To make the Crème Anglaise, heat the milk and vanilla, but don't allow to boil. In a separate bowl, beat the egg yolks and sugar until light and creamy. Gradually whisk the hot milk into the egg mixture. Heat in a double saucepan or bain marie, stirring constantly with a whisk, until mixture thickens and coats the back of a spoon. Remove vanilla bean, if using, and transfer the mixture to a bowl. Cover and refrigerate until ready to use. This mixture can be refrigerated for up to 3 days.

Cardamom-scented Orange Salad

Serves 4

615 kilojoules/**145** calories per serve; **3.5g** total fat; **0.2g** saturated fat; **20mg** sodium

4 large firm navel oranges (or Valencia if
  out of season)
1 tablespoon orange flower water
1 tablespoon sugar
1 teaspoon cardamom seeds
  (or 4–5 cardamom pods, split)
6–8 fresh mint leaves
4 dates, pitted and sliced
2 tablespoons flaked almonds, toasted

Honey Yoghurt

⅓ cup low-fat yoghurt
few drops vanilla essence
1–2 teaspoons honey, gently warmed to
  soften

Peel and slice the oranges. Arrange in a layer in a flat bowl and sprinkle with the orange flower water, sugar and cardamom seeds. Cover and refrigerate overnight.

Combine the yoghurt, vanilla and honey in a small bowl and mix well.

To serve, remove cardamom seeds and place orange slices on plates.

Scatter with the mint, dates and almonds and serve with the honey yoghurt.

Champagne and Watermelon Jellies

Serves 6 adults

555 kilojoules/**130** calories per serve; **0.1g** total fat; **0g** saturated fat; **25mg** sodium

1½ sachets (1½ tablespoons) gelatine
⅓ cup caster sugar
½ cup water
625ml (2½ cups) sparkling wine or champagne
1 cup pureed watermelon or rockmelon

Combine gelatine, sugar and water in a medium saucepan and stir over low heat until sugar dissolves. Take care not to let mixture boil. Remove from heat and add the champagne and watermelon. Pour into one large serving bowl or individual cups and refrigerate until jelly has set.

Gelato Duo – Rockmelon and Pistachio

Serves 4

1805 kilojoules/**430** calories per serve; **23g** total fat; **4.1g** saturated fat; **80mg** sodium

Ices are one of the world's favourite desserts and with this low-fat recipe you can indulge freely. The list of substitutes for the rockmelon is endless: try any other kind of melon, such as watermelon or honeydew, or berries, such as raspberry, blueberry, young berry, strawberry or gooseberry. You could also choose fruits such as persimmon, lychee, nectarine, peach, apricot, cherry, mango, plum, rambutan, banana, guava, fig, kiwi, passionfruit, pineapple or pawpaw.

Base mix for each gelato
- 500ml (2 cups) skim or low-fat milk
- 4 egg yolks
- 125g caster sugar

Rockmelon gelato
- 2 cups puréed fresh rockmelon

Pistachio gelato
- 125g pistachios, finely ground, or try hazelnuts, plus extra chopped pistachios, to serve

To make the base, heat the milk until near boiling point but don't boil. Beat the egg yolks and sugar in a large bowl until thick and creamy. Add a few spoons of the hot milk while beating, then gradually add the remainder in a thin stream. Transfer mixture to a double boiler or bain marie and cook, whisking until mixture coats the back of a spoon. Don't allow the custard to boil. Pour into a jug, cover and chill. This can be kept for a few days before making gelato.

Pour mixture into an ice-cream churn – after 1–2 minutes churning, add either the rockmelon or ground pistachio nuts, and make the gelato following manufacturer's instructions.

If you don't own an ice-cream churn, beat the custard and flavouring together, pour into ice cube trays and freeze. Transfer to a food processor and beat well to break up the crystals then pour into an ice-cream tray. When nearly frozen, beat again then repeat this process 3–4 times over the next 1–2 hours to make as smooth as possible.

Serve with extra chopped pistachios.

Free-form Apricot and Almond Tarts

Makes 8 tarts

1305 kilojoules/**310** calories per serve; **10g** total fat; **1.1g** saturated fat; **330mg** sodium

When apricots are in season, these tarts may be made with the fresh variety. Make sure they're entirely ripe and juicy. Nectarines may be substituted.

Almond paste – also known as frangipane – is a classic component for tarts, in particular fruit tarts. Not only does it contribute fantastic flavour with great depth, the layer between the pastry and the fruit ensures that the pastry does not become soggy during baking.

425g can apricots in natural juice

Bases

2½ cups self-raising flour

2 tablespoons sugar

½ cup low-fat apricot or plain yoghurt

½ cup low-fat milk

2 tablespoons light olive or canola oil

Almond Paste

1 eggwhite, lightly beaten

½ cup ground almonds

2 tablespoons sugar, plus

1–2 teaspoons extra

few drops almond essence

Preheat oven to 180°C.

Drain the apricots well and dice.

To make the bases, sift the flour and sugar into a bowl. Whisk together the yoghurt, milk and oil and pour into the flour. Mix quickly and lightly to a soft dough. Turn onto a floured board and knead gently until smooth. Wrap in plastic and refrigerate 10 minutes.

Reserve 1 tablespoon of the eggwhite. Combine the remainder with the almonds, sugar and essence and mix to a paste.

To make tarts, roll the dough to 3–4mm thickness and cut into 14–15cm rounds. Place a spoon of the paste on the centre of each disc and spread out, leaving a 2cm border. Top with a spoon of the apricots. Bring dough edges over the apricots, pleating the edges and pinching to hold in place. Brush with reserved eggwhite and sprinkle with extra sugar. Bake on lined oven trays for 15–20 minutes or until golden brown.

Chilled Fruit Gazpacho with Frozen Banana Crème

Serves 8

660 kilojoules/**155** calories per serve; **0g** total fat; **0g** saturated fat; **25mg** sodium

Try your own creation with this versatile dessert. Kids might like it with sparkling apple juice – let them choose and chop the fruit. For a special dinner party, try red or white wine as the liquid.

1 litre (4 cups) grape or apple juice
500ml (2 cups) water
¼ cup caster sugar
1 cinnamon stick or 3 star anise
zest of ½ lemon
zest of ½ orange
½ cup frozen or fresh raspberries or
  other berries
4 cups chopped seasonal fruit (such as
  kiwi fruit, pineapple, grapes, rockmelon,
  strawberries or other berries)
mint for garnish
Frozen Banana Crème
2 large bananas, peeled and frozen
¼ cup low-fat fruit yoghurt
fresh mint leaves, for garnish

To make soup, place the juice, water, sugar, cinnamon and zests in a large stainless steel saucepan. Bring to the boil, lower heat and simmer gently until mixture has reduced by about half or is starting to become syrupy. Strain and allow to cool. Purée with the raspberries. Divide chopped fruit among serving bowls and spoon over the syrup.

Just before serving, place the frozen bananas in a food processor with the yoghurt and pulse on and off until smooth. Place a spoon of the mixture on the top of each 'soup' with a few slivers or a leaf of mint and serve immediately, before the bananas have a chance to melt.

Green Tea Mousse with Sweet Wonton Crisps

Makes 10 serves

575 kilojoules/**135** calories per serve; **4g** total fat; **2.2g** saturated fat; **85mg** sodium

I've chosen normal evaporated milk in this recipe rather than the reduced-fat variety, because it holds a better froth. It still makes a fairly low-fat dessert compared to its cream counterparts.

2 cups very strong Japanese or Jasmine
  Green Tea (you'll need about 8 tea bags)
½ cup caster sugar
25g (2½ sachets) gelatine
375ml (1½ cups) can evaporated milk
  (see note)
1 teaspoon vanilla essence
few drops green food colouring, optional
Wonton Crisps
6 wonton wrappers, 19 x 19cm
1 egg white, lightly beaten
2 tablespoons caster sugar
1 tablespoon almond or hazelnut meal,
  optional

Place the tea, half the sugar and gelatine in a saucepan and heat without boiling until sugar dissolves. Remove from heat. Using electric beaters, whip the evaporated milk until soft peaks form, gradually add the remaining sugar, vanilla and colouring and beat until sugar has dissolved. Turn to a slow speed and gradually pour in the tea mixture, beating until just incorporated. Allow to sit for 10 minutes, banging a few times on the bench to break up any large air bubbles. Pour into one large glass bowl or individual glasses and refrigerate until set. Serve with a wonton crisp.

To make Wonton Crisps, brush one side lightly with the egg and dust with the sugar and nut meal. Cut in half, diagonally, and place on a lined baking tray. Bake in a moderate oven until crisp and golden, about 10–15 minutes. Store in an airtight container.

Pineapple and Mint Sushi

Serves 6

1225 kilojoules/**295** calories per serve; **4.5g** total fat; **0.7g** saturated fat; **25mg** sodium

This recipe is a little challenging but fun to make and well worth the effort. A real treat for guests. I love it with the Crème Anglaise on page 122 but for a fresh twist try using mint leaves instead of a vanilla bean.

1 cup calrose, arborio or jasmine rice

250ml (1 cup) low-fat milk

¾ cup water

2 tablespoons caster sugar

1 vanilla bean or 1 teaspoon vanilla

2 tablespoons pineapple or apple juice

8 sheets confectioner's rice paper (see note on page 154)

1 bunch mint, large tender leaves picked and washed

½ pineapple, cut into long thin strips

¼ cup lightly toasted almonds, finely crushed

Place rice in a large saucepan, cover with cold water and swish vigorously with your hands. Drain and repeat process until water runs clear. Allow to stand for 10–20 minutes. Combine rice, milk, water, sugar and vanilla in saucepan. Cover and bring to the boil, reduce heat and simmer for 5 minutes, then remove from heat and allow to steam for 20 minutes with the lid on. Don't be tempted to remove the lid during process. Remove vanilla bean.

Using a spatula or flat wooden spoon, cut through the rice with a slicing motion while gradually adding the juice. Fan the rice at the same time to cool it down. The rice should now be quite creamy and solid. Cover with a damp cloth and keep at room temperature.

This next stage needs to be done quickly, as the rice paper softens easily, so make sure you have the fruit already sliced. On a sheet of baking paper, place 2 sheets of rice paper on top of each other, with the long side facing you. Slide the top sheet away from you 6cm, so there is an overlap of about 10cm in the middle. Place a quarter of the rice mixture along the overlapped area, pressing down gently as you would for sushi. Lay mint leaves down centre then top with a line of the pineapple. Bring closest edge of rice paper over the rice, then roll up to make a firm log, using the baking paper to help roll it tightly. Cover tightly in plastic wrap and refrigerate until ready to serve.

To serve, sprinkle almonds over a flat board or sheet of baking paper. Remove plastic from sushi and roll in almonds to coat. Cut diagonally in desired lengths and serve as is, with a fruit purée, or even Lime Mint Sauce on page 136.

Warm Tropical Fruit Salad with Orange Rum Sauce

Serves 4

920 kilojoules/**220** calories per serve; **1.5g** total fat; **0.1g** saturated fat; **10mg** sodium

*Try with
a dollop of thick
yoghurt or a little
shredded coconut.*

2 bananas, halved lengthwise

2 teaspoons lemon juice

1 mango, sliced

4 slices pineapple, halved and cored

1 tablespoon brown sugar

1 teaspoon cinnamon

oil for brushing pan

Orange Rum Sauce

¾ cup orange juice

2 tablespoons rum

2 tablespoons brown sugar

Brush the banana with the lemon juice, then toss all the fruit in the sugar and cinnamon. Set aside.

To make the Orange Rum Sauce, combine the orange juice, rum and brown sugar in a small saucepan and bring to the boil. Reduce heat and simmer until the mixture thickens to a sauce consistency, about 15 minutes. Keep warm.

Heat a grill pan or non-stick pan and brush with oil. Add the fruit and cook 2–3 minutes on each side or until golden brown and heated through. Serve with the sauce spooned over.

Berry and Apple Pastries

Makes 8 pieces

545 kilojoules/**130** calories per serve; **3g** total fat; **0.6g** saturated fat; **125mg** sodium

*Try sprinkling this
with a little
mixed icing sugar
and cocoa just
before serving.*

3 cups fresh diced apples and mixed berries – try strawberries, raspberries, blueberries

2 tablespoons ground roasted hazelnuts

1 tablespoon liqueur of choice or orange blossom water

2 tablespoons cocoa

2 tablespoons caster sugar

8 sheets filo pastry

Fruit Custard

½ cup low-fat custard

¼ cup fruit purée – try mango or raspberry

Preheat the oven to 220°C.

Toss the fruit with the ground nuts and liqueur. In a separate bowl, combine the cocoa and sugar.

Lay a sheet of filo pastry on a clean dry surface and dust lightly with the cocoa mixture. Top with another sheet and dust again. Repeat with another 2 sheets leaving the top sheet undusted. Cut the pastry stack into 4 crosswise.

Divide fruit mixture between pastries, laying it down one short side and leaving 2cm at each end. Roll up into fingers, tucking in the ends. Repeat process with remaining pastry and fruit. Place on a paper-lined baking tray and bake for 8–10 minutes or until golden brown.

Combine the custard and fruit purée. Serve pastries on flat plates with the custard spooned around the outside.

Banana and Mango Clafouti

Serves 4

1520 kilojoules/**365** calories per serve; **6.5g** total fat; **3.2g** saturated fat; **105mg** sodium

2 large ripe bananas, sliced lengthwise

2 teaspoons lemon juice

¼ cup brown sugar

2 tablespoons cornflour

2 tablespoons brandy

2 mangoes, sliced

Topping

¼ cup sugar, plus 1 tablespoon extra

2 tablespoons flour

2 eggs

½ cup ricotta cheese

¼ cup low-fat milk

1 teaspoon vanilla essence

Preheat oven to 200°C.

Toss the banana in the lemon juice, sugar, cornflour and brandy. Place half in a single layer in 4 lightly-oiled ovenproof dishes or one large dish. Top with a layer of the mango and finish with the remaining banana.

To make the topping, place the sugar, flour, eggs, ricotta, milk and vanilla in a blender and blend until smooth. Pour over the fruit and bake for 25–30 minutes or until set and lightly browned. Sprinkle with extra sugar and place under a hot grill for 1–2 minutes or until browned. Serve while hot.

Papaya and Kiwi Compote with Lime Mint Sauce

Serves 6

505 kilojoules/**120** calories per serve (includes yoghurt); **2g** total fat; **1.1g** saturated fat; **40mg** sodium

Papaya seeds are great for digestion, so set a few aside. When puréed they add a lovely sharp, peppery touch to savoury dressings.

1 papaya (about 400g)

6 kiwi fruit

¼ cup thick natural yoghurt, to serve, optional

Lime Mint Sauce

juice of 1 lime

1 teaspoon grated lime zest

¼ cup water

2 tablespoons caster sugar

¼ cup chopped mint

To make the Lime Mint Sauce, heat the lime juice, zest, water and sugar in a small saucepan and cook over a low heat until the sugar dissolves. Cook for 5 minutes, then cool and purée with the mint leaves.

Remove the seeds from the papaya (see note). Peel and slice both fruits and arrange on plates or a platter. Drizzle with the Lime Mint Sauce and serve plain or with thick natural yoghurt.

Orange and Pecan Biscotti (page 140)

baking

Orange and Pecan Biscotti

Makes 30 biscotti

285 kilojoules/**70** calories per serve; **2.5g** total fat; **0.3g** saturated fat; **15mg** sodium

1¾ cups plain flour

½ teaspoon baking powder

2 large eggs

½ cup caster sugar

1 teaspoon vanilla essence

2 teaspoons grated orange rind

¾ cup pecan nuts

eggwhite for brushing

Preheat oven to 180°C.

Sift the flour and baking powder into a large bowl. Set aside. Using electric mixers, beat the eggs and sugar until thick and doubled in bulk. Beat in the vanilla and orange rind. Gently fold into the flour, together with the pecans. Transfer to a well-floured board and knead gently until smooth. Divide in quarters and shape each into a 20cm log. Lay on baking paper-lined baking trays, brush with eggwhite and bake for 15–20 minutes or until golden brown and firm. Allow to cool for 10 minutes, then slice diagonally into 1cm slices.

Turn oven down to 160°C.

Lay biscuits flat on baking trays and bake for 20–25 minutes or until dry and crisp. Cool on a wire rack before storing in an airtight container.

Guinness Fruit Cake

Makes a 30cm loaf or a 25cm round cake (16 slices)

1190 kilojoules/**285** calories per serve; **9g** total fat; **1.2g** saturated fat; **245mg** sodium

250ml (1 cup) Guinness stout

¾ cup molasses or treacle

1 teaspoon bicarbonate of soda

1 tablespoon grated ginger

375g mixed dried fruit

2 cups self-raising flour

2 teaspoons mixed spice

3 eggs

¾ cup brown sugar

½ cup light olive or canola oil

Preheat oven to 180°C. Grease and line a cake tin with baking paper.

In a large saucepan, bring the stout and molasses to the boil (take care as it foams up). Remove from the heat, add the bicarbonate of soda, ginger and dried fruit. Cover and allow mixture to cool to room temperature.

Combine the flour and mixed spice.

In a large bowl, beat the eggs and sugar until thick and creamy. Gradually add the oil while beating. Gently fold the beer and flour mixtures alternately into the eggs, ending with the flour. Spoon mixture into prepared tin and bake for 1 hour or until a skewer inserted in the centre comes out clean and cake springs back when touched. Allow to cool in tin for 10 minutes before turning on to a wire rack.

Guinness Fruit Cake

Fresh Rhubarb and Buttermilk Cake

Makes two 7 x 13cm cakes, or a 24cm cake (12 slices)
1510 kilojoules/**360** calories per serve; **7g** total fat; **1.1g** saturated fat; **230mg** sodium

This cake is delicious just plain iced, but its slightly puddingy consistency also makes it ideal as a warm dessert served with the reserved syrup.

Although people think of rhubarb as a fruit, it is actually a vegetable. Its leaves are poisonous – they contain oxalic acid – and should be removed as soon as you bring the bunch home.

3 cups chopped rhubarb
½ cup water
½ cup orange juice
1 cup sugar
3 eggs
¼ cup oil
½ cup well-shaken buttermilk
2½ cups self-raising flour
1 teaspoon ginger

Buttermilk and Orange Icing
2 cups icing sugar
grated rind of ½ orange
1 teaspoon orange juice
2–3 tablespoons well-shaken buttermilk

Preheat oven to 180°C. Lightly oil and flour two 7 x 13cm cake tins or one 24cm cake tin.

Combine the rhubarb, water, juice and half of the sugar in a saucepan and bring to the boil. Reduce heat and simmer for 10 minutes or until rhubarb is tender. Allow to cool in liquid. Strain, reserving liquid. Mash rhubarb, adding back enough liquid to measure 1½ cups purée.

If there is any remaining liquid, it can be boiled to reduce and thicken, and served as a syrup with the cake/s, if desired (see note).

With electric mixers beat the eggs with the remaining ½ cup sugar until thick and creamy. Gradually add the oil and buttermilk, while beating. Sift together the flour and ginger and gently fold ⅓ through the batter. Fold through half of the rhubarb, then repeat, so flour is the last addition. Spoon into prepared tin/s and bake for 35 minutes or until a skewer inserted into the centre comes out clean.

To make icing, beat together the icing sugar, orange juice and enough buttermilk to make a spreadable consistency. Spread on the cake/s when cool.

Hazelnut and Ginger Meringues

Makes about 48 meringues

255 kilojoules/**60** calories per meringue; **4g** total fat; **0.2g** saturated fat; **5mg** sodium

1 cup roughly chopped roasted hazelnuts
1¼ cups caster sugar
3 eggwhites
pinch of cream of tartar
2 teaspoons finely diced glace ginger
1 teaspoon ginger powder
48 whole raw hazelnuts

Preheat oven to 120°C.

Combine the chopped hazelnuts and ¼ cup of the caster sugar in a food processor until finely chopped. In a separate bowl beat the eggwhites and cream of tartar until soft peaks form.

Gradually beat in the remaining cup of sugar until sugar has dissolved and mixture is stiff. Fold in the hazelnut and sugar mixture and the glace and powdered ginger.

Place heaped teaspoons of mixture on oven trays lined with baking paper, allowing room for spreading, and top each with a whole hazelnut. Bake for 40–45 minutes or until dry and crisp, but not browned.

Oat Bars

Makes 24 bars

445 kilojoules/**105** calories per serve; **3.5g** total fat; **0.6g** saturated fat; **20mg** sodium

3 cups rolled oats
1 cup finely diced dried apricots or peaches
¾ cup sugar
⅓ cup slivered almonds
1 teaspoon cinnamon
¼ cup water
½ cup low-fat apricot yoghurt
2 tablespoons melted margarine
1 tablespoon sesame seeds

Preheat oven to 190°C. Line a 21 x 30cm lamington tin with baking paper.

Combine the oats, apricots, sugar, almonds and cinnamon in a bowl. Lightly beat the water, yoghurt and margarine, pour over and mix well to combine. This can also be mixed in a food processor, but don't overbeat.

Press mixture into prepared tin, sprinkle with sesame seeds and mark into 24 bars. Bake for 20 minutes or until crisp and golden-brown. Cool in pan on a wire rack, then store in an airtight container for up to 2 weeks. Suitable for freezing.

Lemongrass and Lime Sponge

Makes a 22cm cake (12 slices)

1105 kilojoules/**265** calories per serve; **5g** total fat; **2.4g** saturated fat; **210mg** sodium

Ground lemongrass can be found in most supermarkets. If you can't find it, chop 1 tablespoon fresh lemongrass very finely and boil for 10 minutes in 100ml water. Allow to steep for 10 minutes, strain and use this as the hot water for the sponge mix.

Fresh lemongrass is often found in Thai dishes. The bottom part of the stem is used only, and the first few layers are removed to reveal the tender core. The core is very finely sliced and added to salads, or bruised to release flavours and pounded in a mortar to be added to curry pastes.

3 eggs, separated
¾ cup caster sugar
1 teaspoon grated lime zest
1 cup self-raising flour
1 teaspoon ground lemongrass (see note)
3 tablespoons hot water

Lime Cream

125g (½ cup) low-fat ricotta cheese
85g (⅓ cup) light cream cheese
¾ cup icing sugar
grated zest of ½ lime
1 teaspoon lime juice

Preheat oven to 180°C. Grease and flour a 22cm cake tin.

Beat the eggwhites until stiff peaks form. Gradually add the sugar and continue beating until dissolved. Add the yolks and lime zest and beat just to combine. Sift together the flour and lemongrass and gently fold through the egg mixture followed by the water.

Spoon mixture into prepared tin and bake for 20–25 minutes or until golden and cake springs back when pressed gently. Leave in tin for 5–10 minutes before turning onto a wire rack to cool. Cut sponge in half and fill with the lime cream. Sprinkle top with icing sugar.

To make Lime Cream, place all ingredients in a bowl and beat with an electric mixer until thick and creamy.

Bush Damper with Australian Dukkah

Makes 12 large wedges of damper and 1 cup of dukkah
Damper: 460 kilojoules/**110** calories per serve; **2.5g** total fat; **0.6g** saturated fat; **175mg** sodium
Dukkah: 320 kilojoules/**75** calories per cup; **8g** total fat; **0.9g** saturated fat; **0mg** sodium

Meditteranean dukkah usually uses coriander, cumin, sesame seeds and hazelnuts, so if you're reluctant to try the Australian version, give that one a go.

Damper
2 cups self-raising flour
1 tablespoon wattle seeds (or linseed)
1 teaspoon lemon myrtle
1 teaspoon native mountain pepper
250ml (1 cup) well-shaken buttermilk
1 tablespoon macadamia or olive oil
milk for brushing dough

Dukkah Mixture
½ cup chopped macadamia nuts
¼ cup chopped hazelnuts
1 tablespoon ground bush tomato
1 teaspoon lemon myrtle
1 teaspoon mountain pepper
1 teaspoon native aniseed

Preheat oven to 180°C.

Sift the flour and seasonings into a large bowl and make a well in the centre. Combine the buttermilk and oil and pour into the well. Mix quickly and lightly to a soft dough, then turn onto a floured board and knead until smooth. Shape into a cob (a round loaf shape) and place on a lined or lightly oiled baking tray. Brush with milk and bake for 40–50 minutes or until golden brown and hollow sounding when tapped. Serve with macadamia or extra virgin olive oil and the Dukkah for dipping.

To make Dukkah Mixture, place chopped macadamias and chopped hazelnuts on a roasting pan and bake in a moderate oven until golden brown. Grind, then toss with ground bush tomato, lemon myrtle, mountain pepper and native aniseed. Return to oven and bake until mixture becomes aromatic. This can also be done on the stove top in a non-stick pan, but take care not to burn the herb mixture.

This can be stored in an airtight container for 1–2 weeks, or longer in the freezer. Try sprinkling on salads, steamed rice, pasta and meat or fish dishes for a tasty Australian touch.

Raisin and Currant Tea Bread

Makes a 22cm round cake or a 13 x 21cm loaf (20 slices)

655 kilojoules/**155** calories per serve; **2.5g** total fat; **0.3g** saturated fat; **115mg** sodium

This is delicious either plain or spread with fresh ricotta cheese.

1 cup raisins

1½ cup currants

375ml (1½ cups) cold strong Earl Grey or Lady Grey tea

1 tablespoon treacle

1 egg, lightly beaten

¾ cup brown sugar

2 cups self-raising flour, sifted

1 teaspoon mixed spice

½ cup walnuts

Place the fruits in a large bowl, pour over the tea and stir in the treacle. Cover and allow to soak overnight.

Preheat oven to 160°C and line a 22cm round tin with baking paper.

Stir beaten egg into fruit mixture followed by the sugar, then the sifted flour, spice and walnuts. Spoon into prepared tin and bake for 1–1¼ hours or until a skewer inserted in the centre comes out clean. Allow to cool for 10 minutes in tin on a wire rack before turning out.

Chocolate and Orange Cake

Makes 12 regular muffins, or a 24cm cake (12 slices)

945 kilojoules/**225** calories per muffin; **13g** total fat; **2.5g** saturated fat; **130mg** sodium

3 eggs

½ cup firmly packed brown sugar

⅓ cup olive oil

½ cup mashed pie apple (or cooked apple purée)

1 tablespoon grated orange zest

1 cup self-raising flour

½ cup almond meal

½ cup cocoa

100ml well-shaken buttermilk

icing sugar, for dusting

Preheat the oven to 180°C. Lightly oil or spray the muffin tins or the cake tin.

Beat the eggs and sugar with electric beaters until thick and creamy. Gradually add the oil while beating, followed by the apple and grated zest. Sift together the flour, almond meal and cocoa and lightly fold half through the batter. Stir in the buttermilk, then fold through the remaining flour mixture until just combined. Spoon into prepared muffin tins or cake tin, and bake for 15–20 minutes for the muffins, or 35–40 minutes for the cake, or until a skewer inserted in the centre comes out clean. Allow to cool in tin for 10 minutes before turning out on a wire rack to cool completely. If preferred, dust with icing sugar before serving.

Pistachio and Carrot Cake

Makes a 20cm square cake (16 squares)

1295 kilojoules/**310** calories per serve; **9.5g** total fat; **1.7g** saturated fat; **235mg** sodium

You may have noticed a lot of nuts used in this book and wonder why. Many people don't realise that all nuts are healthy. They contain valuable nutrients and the oils are mainly mono- or poly-unsaturated, the preferred type for good health. (Coconut is the exception as it has more saturated fat). I often use nuts to replace some of the texture and flavour lost when creating low-fat recipes – they add a lot of interest to a recipe. Be creative and experiment with your favourite nuts. The only caution: if you are watching your weight, use nuts instead of other fats, not in addition to.

2 cups self-raising flour
½ cup wholemeal self-raising flour
½ teaspoon bicarbonate of soda
1 teaspoon cinnamon
1 teaspoon nutmeg
½ cup raisins
¾ cup roughly chopped unsalted roasted pistachio nuts, or preferred nuts (see note)
1½ cups grated carrot
½ cup brown sugar
⅓ cup canola oil
2 eggs
½ cup well-shaken buttermilk
225g crushed pineapple, drained

Icing
2 cups icing sugar, sifted
¼ cup light cream cheese
2 teaspoons grated lemon rind
1 teaspoon lemon juice

Preheat oven to 180ºC. Lightly oil and flour, or line a 20cm square cake tin with baking paper.

Sift the flours, soda and spices into a large bowl. Toss through the raisins, nuts and carrot. In a separate bowl, beat the sugar and oil until light and fluffy. While still beating, add the eggs, one at a time, beating well after each addition, then stir in the buttermilk. Pour into the flour mixture with the pineapple and stir lightly to make a batter.

Spoon into prepared tin and bake for 25–35 minutes or until a skewer inserted in the centre comes out clean. Allow to cool for 10 minutes in tin before turning onto a wire rack to cool. When cold, spread with icing and, if desired, decorate with finely chopped pistachios.

To make icing, place all ingredients in a bowl and mix well. Gradually add a little boiling water a few drops at a time, to bring to spreading consistency.

Citrus Panforte

Makes about 40 pieces

290 kilojoules/**70** calories per serve; **4.5g** total fat; **0.4g** saturated fat; **0mg** sodium

Confectioner's rice paper can be found in most health food stores, European delicatessens and well-stocked supermarkets. Don't confuse it with the Asian rice paper.

confectioner's rice paper for lining tin
  (see note)
1 cup almonds
1 cup walnuts or macadamia nuts
1 cup mixed peel
½ cup glace ginger (or preferred glace fruit)
1 tablespoon grated orange rind
1 teaspoon grated lemon rind
1 teaspoon ground cinnamon
1 teaspoon mixed spice
pinch ground white pepper
½ cup plain flour
½ cup honey
⅓ cup sugar

Preheat oven to 180°C. Line the base of a 22cm square tin with the rice paper, and line the sides of the tin with baking paper.

Combine the nuts, mixed peel, ginger, rinds, spices and flour in a large bowl. Mix well.

Warm the honey and sugar in a saucepan over low heat until the sugar dissolves, brushing down sides of pan with a brush dipped in hot water to stop sugar sticking. Bring to the boil, reduce heat and simmer for 6–8 minutes or until mixture forms a soft ball when dropped in a glass of cold water. Immediately mix through the fruit mixture, stirring well, to combine thoroughly.

Spoon into prepared tin and flatten top, pushing mixture out to the edges. Bake for 30–35 minutes. Allow to cool in tin on a wire rack. When cool, mark into squares and dust with icing sugar if desired.

Sweet Potato Wedges

Makes 10 wedges

810 kilojoules/**195** calories per serve; **5.5g** total fat; **2.3g** saturated fat; **255mg** sodium

2 cups self-raising flour
1 teaspoon mixed spice
¾ cup cold mashed sweet potato
  (the orange variety)
1 tablespoon brown sugar
150ml low-fat milk
1 tablespoon canola or light olive oil
low-fat milk, extra, for brushing
Apricot Ricotta Whip
1 cup fresh ricotta cheese
1 teaspoon vanilla essence
½ cup dried apricots, soaked for
  1 hour to soften, drained and chopped
1 tablespoon icing sugar

Preheat oven to 190°C. Lightly oil or spray a baking tray or line with baking paper.

Sift the flour and mixed spice into a large bowl. In a separate bowl or blender, beat together the mashed sweet potato, sugar, milk and oil until smooth. Pour into the flour and mix quickly and lightly with a butter knife to a soft dough. Turn on to a floured board and knead gently until smooth. Shape into a 20cm circle and place on prepared tray. Mark into wedges and brush top with milk. Bake for 20 minutes or until golden brown. Serve warm or cold with the apricot ricotta whip.

To make apricot ricotta whip, beat all the ingredients together until light and fluffy with electric beaters or in a food processor.

focus on flavour

Everyone wants to get pleasure from the food they eat, so

there's no point in changing the way you eat if you're not

going to enjoy it. If you simply want to start eating better for

your long-term health, and still enjoy the great pleasures

food has to offer, remember that flavour, along with visual

appeal and texture, are so very important. Life is too short to

go on bland, uninteresting diets.

Here are a few ideas to help you liven up your meals.

from the east

rice wine vinegar For a light, clean flavour that adds mild acidity. Adds a lift to rice, salads, Asian-style marinades, or splash on fish.

mirin A blend of rice wine and sugar that adds a subtle sweetness and bouquet to dishes, dressings, stir-fries and marinades.

sesame oil Just a few drops are all that's needed to add a rich and aromatic flavour to dishes. Great in marinades, stir-fries and just tossed through rice, or in salad dressings. It is powerful, though, so go a drop at a time or dilute in milder oils or vinegar.

fish sauce For a fresh, aromatic touch of the sea, only a touch is needed. Add to stocks or the cooking liquid for Asian soups. It's high in salt, though, so go easy if you're watching your sodium intake.

kaffir lime leaves This ingredient adds a pungent, lime-like aura when added to the cooking liquid of rice, soups, noodles, ravioli. Also use crumbled in casseroles and baked fish or chicken dishes.

hoisin and oyster sauce A change from the usual soy, hoisin is sweet and spicy and great as a glaze or marinade. Oyster sauce is made from oyster water and salt and adds a rich, characteristic element to dishes. Both are fairly high in salt – look for the ones without MSG.

dried mushrooms For a rich, smoky mushroom flavour, add to cooking water of soups, rice, noodles, or just soak to soften and toss through stir-fries and salads.

ginger An indispensable ingredient that is not only good for your health, but incredibly versatile – from the fresh root chopped in stir-fries, to pickled for sushi, or tossed through salads, rice or sauces, or even the piquant glazed ginger for adding zing to cakes and baking.

lemongrass An aromatic, citrus flavour for a huge range of dishes. Try lemongrass chopped fresh, dried, preserved or even ground.

wasabi If sinus-clearing heat is what you're after, use it in abundance. For a more subtle, fresh bite to sauces, rice or spreads, use just a touch of this Japanese horseradish.

from the west

balsamic vinegar A rich, dark and slightly sweet vinegar used for centuries by Italians in salad dressings, marinades, glazes, splashed over fish and meat, or just added to olive oil for dipping bread.

extra virgin olive oil Loaded with the valuable monounsaturates, olive oil may be high in fat, as all oils are, but a good-quality, fruity extra virgin olive oil will go a long way and bring a wonderful aromatic flavour to food cooked in it or salads dressed with it. It's well worth the investment on your health and pleasure and one of the healthiest things to have with your bread.

nut oils Macadamia, hazelnut, walnut and other nut oils all have a distinctive flavour and can add a new dimension to your cooking. Taste and experiment for yourself.

tomato paste Look for the one with no added salt as, being concentrated, the natural salt of the tomato speaks for itself. Add to cold or hot pasta sauces, dressings and rice dishes. Tomato paste also adds a rich, full element to low-fat stews and casseroles, or when added to meat or onion when sautéeing and allowed to turn a rust colour and become aromatic.

mustard Whether wholegrain, Dijon, hot English, honey, or any of the huge range available, mustard adds a distinct flavour and richness to sandwiches, dressings, or spread over meat and roasts. It's fairly high in salt.

fresh herbs There's nothing that gives dishes quite the lift that fresh herbs do. Experiment to find your own favourite food-and-herb combinations, whether tossed through salad, sauces, pasta, rice, soup, as a "crust" for fish and meat, or just chopped and added to a simple sandwich.

nuts and seeds Another food abounding in monounsaturated and polyunsaturated oils. Use as a crunchy surprise in texture and flavour in salads, sandwiches, through rice and pasta, ground or chopped on meat, or through breads and cakes. For extra flavour and richness, toast or dry roast before using.

measurements and conversions

imperial/metric conversion chart

Metric cup and spoon sizes

Measurements used in this book refer to the standard metric cup and spoon sets approved by the Standards Association of Australia. A basic metric cup set consists of: 1 cup, ½ cup, ⅓ cup and ¼ cup sizes. The basic spoon set comprises 1 tablespoon, 1 teaspoon, ½ teaspoon, ¼ teaspoon.

Cup	Spoon
¼ cup = 60ml	¼ teaspoon = 1.25ml
⅓ cup = 80ml	½ teaspoon = 2.5ml
½ cup = 125ml	1 teaspoon = 5ml
1 cup = 250ml	1 tablespoon = 20ml

Liquids

Imperial	Metric	Metric
1fl oz	-	30 ml
2fl oz	¼ cup	60ml
3fl oz	-	100ml
4fl oz	½ cup	125ml
5fl oz	-	150ml
6fl oz	¾ cup	200ml
8fl oz	1 cup	250ml
10fl oz	1¼ cups	300ml
12fl oz	1½ cups	375ml
14 fl oz	1¾ cups	425ml
15fl oz	-	475ml
16fl oz	2 cups	500ml
20fl oz (1 pint)	2½ cups	600ml

Mass (weight)

(Approximate conversion for cookery purposes)

Imperial	Metric	Imperial	Metric
½oz	15g	10oz	315g
1oz	30g	11oz	345g
2oz	60g	12oz (¾ lb)	375g
3oz	90g	13oz	410g
4oz (¼ lb)	125g	14oz	440g
5oz	155g	15oz	470g
6oz	185g	16oz (1lb)	500g (0.5kg)
7oz	220g	24oz (1½lb)	750g
8oz (½ lb)	250g	32oz (2lb)	1000g (1kg)
9oz	280g	3lb	1500g (1.5kg)

Oven temperatures

Oven	Fahrenheit	Celsius
Very slow	250°	120°
Slow	275–300°	140–150°
Moderately slow	325°	160°
Moderate	350°	180°
Moderately hot	375°	190°
Hot	400–450°	200–230°
Very hot	475–500°	250–260°

Note: For fan ovens set approximately 20° Celsius below the stated temperature.

index